Stumbling into Film History

To dear, sweet Amanda
  Love,
   Lon

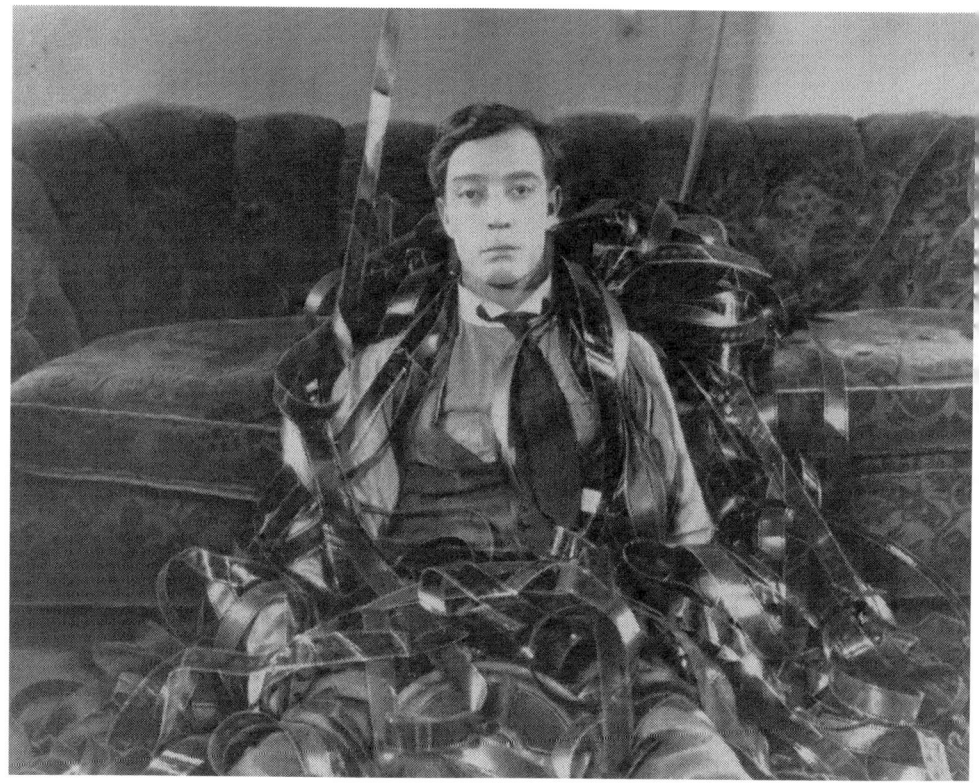

Stumbling into Film History

Lon Davis

Stumbling Into Film History:
©2024 Lon & Debra Davis

No part of this book may be reproduced in any form or by any means, whether by electronic, mechanical, or digital, or through photocopying or recording, except for brief excerpts included in reviews, without permission in writing from the publisher.

Printed in the United States of America
Library of Congress Cataloguing in Publication Data:
Stumbling Into Film History
Paperback ISBN 979-8-88771-383-0
Case ISBN 979-8-88771-384-7
Supervising editor and consultant: Debra L. Davis.
Copyeditor: Scott H. Reboul.
Cover photos courtesy of Scott MacGillivray and Steve Massa.
The back cover photo was taken by Greg Burns for *Eugene Magazine*. *Reprinted by permission.*

Published in the USA by:
BearManor Media
1317 Edgewater Dr #110
Orlando, FL 32804
www.bearmanormedia.com

BearManor Media, Orlando, Florida
Printed in the United States of America
Book design by Robbie Adkins, www.adkinsconsult.com

To author and scholar
MARK PRUETT
A dear friend and a stimulating conversationalist,
particularly on the subject of film.

Table of Contents

Acknowledgments viii

Foreword x

Introduction xiii

One: Beverly Bayne: Star of the Silent Films 1

Two: The MPTF: There's No Place Like the Home 23

Three: Mary MacLaren: A Petal on the Current 63

Four: Bob Chatterton: Underfoot in Hollywood 85

Five: Eddie LeVeque: The Last of the Keystone Kops 103

Six: Buster Keaton: Saluting *The General*. 119

Seven: Zoe Rae: The Universal Baby. 135

Eight: Kevin Brownlow: The Humble Historian. 153

Nine: Baby Peggy: The Last Silent Star. 173

Ten: Finding Our Niche: A Love Story. 195

Index: 214

Acknowledgments

I may live in the past, but I have some wonderful friends in the present.

Scott H. Reboul, my aide-de-camp, is always there for me, looking up phone numbers and addresses of obscure movie people, providing me with just the right picture for just the right subject; proofreading my final drafts; and ever-so-diplomatically offering his invaluable feedback on every phase of the writing process.

Pancho Kohner, my friend and collaborator, is a true gentleman and Hollywood insider. He kindly provided the foreword to this book.

Benjamin Ohmart, my indulgent publisher, continues to believe in me as I do in him.

Robbie Adkins, my favorite designer, whose vast experience has made her that rare and wonderful combination of creative and collaborative.

I am also fortunate to know some of the world's most prolific collectors of early film memorabilia, who also happen to be generous with their time, knowledge, and materials. They are Kevin Brownlow, Steve Cox, Michael Campino, Scott MacGillivray, Jerry Murbach, Steve Massa, Michael J. Hayde, Chris Seguin, Brent Walker, John Bengtson, Mitchell Hadley, David Kiehn, Ted Okuda, Sam Gill, James Robert Parish, Leonard Maltin, Randy Skretvedt, Tim Lussier, Lea Stans, Paul E. Gierucki, Marc Wanamaker, and the late (and greatly missed) Cole Johnson and Larry Telles.

On the promotion side, I deeply appreciate podcast interviewers Stu Shostak, Richard Skipper, Phil Hall, and Jordan Rich for providing me with a forum to talk about my projects.

If you've ever wondered Whatever Became of Richard Lamparski, I'm pleased to report that he has survived into his nineties and currently resides in Santa Barbara, California. Mr. Lamparski's fascinating books were pivotal to my quest in contacting stars of the past. I was able to thank him for this during a lengthy phone conversation we had in 2011.

Thanks are also due our good friend Daniel Harrell of Forest Lawn-Glendale, Trisha Schoenberg of *Eugene Magazine*, Mary Huelsbeck of the Wisconsin Center for Film and Theatre Research, Emma Stoltenberg of the Arizona State Library Archives and Public Records, and Jeff Benziger of *The Turlock Journal*. Another invaluable resource is the Media History Digital Library. This online collection provides instant access to vintage trade journals that were once as elusive as the Dead Sea Scrolls.

Finally, I offer my profound appreciation to my extraordinary partner of forty-five years, Debra LaCoe Davis. Deb was my consultant on this (and every) project, listening and making pertinent, insightful cuts and additions as I read each draft aloud. Simply put, she is my past, present, and future.

L.D.

Foreword

Before the glitz and glamour of the "talkies," silent films ruled the screen, relying solely on riveting images and actors' expressive faces to tell a story. Title cards provided context, while live musicians added a dash of drama right in the theatre. Silent films were nothing short of a visual feast, a sophisticated dance of storytelling that captivated audiences far and wide.

Here, in his latest book, Lon Davis shares deeply personal stories of his early years as a burgeoning film historian. With a contagious passion for silent films and a knack for making history seem like a fun family reunion, Lon writes about his friendships with some of the early movies' biggest stars.

Remember Beverly Bayne, the brunette beauty of the silent screen? Well, Lon does. He was just a teenager when he befriended her, learning about her career and her troubled relationship with her leading man and husband, the legendary matinee idol Francis X. Bushman. (The story is so compelling that Lon would later co-write a book and direct a documentary film about it.) Lon also interviewed the once-heralded tragedienne Mary MacLaren, and even had a heart-to-heart with the incredible child star Zoe Rae when she was ninety-five years old. Then there was Diana Serra Cary, a.k.a. Baby Peggy, who took the world by storm, from making millions to facing financial hardship, her story is a roller coaster ride of stratospheric highs and soul-crushing lows. But Lon was there to put a smile on her face, sharing her legacy in his silent film showings and forging a friendship that spanned generations.

Indulging his love of slapstick comedy, Lon spent hilarious and touching moments with Larry Fine of The Three Stooges. He visited Babe London, a comedienne who worked with everyone from Laurel & Hardy to Charlie Chaplin. And he conducted memorable interviews with two of Mack Sennett's original Keystone Kops. These legends were just as thrilled to share their stories with Lon as he was to hear them. Each lovingly written encounter is a testament to Lon's unique ability to connect with these fascinating individuals and bring their stories to life.

Alongside his partner and fellow film enthusiast, Debra, he also shares a love story like no other, intertwining their own romantic tale with that of film pioneers.

So, buckle up, dear reader! You're in for a ride full of laughter, nostalgia, and the undeniable charm of Lon Davis. *Stumbling into Film History* isn't just a book; it's an unforgettable adventure through the golden age of cinema, with the best guide you could ask for.

Pancho Kohner

Lon Davis and Pancho Kohner, Los Angeles, August 2019. Photo by Dr. Margaret Olsen.

Pancho Kohner is a member of Hollywood royalty. His father, Paul Kohner, was a producer and an international talent agent; his mother, Lupita Tovar, was the beautiful Mexican actress who starred in the classic Spanish-language *Drácula* (1931); his uncle was Frederick Kohner, the novelist and screenwriter; his sister is Susan Kohner, the acclaimed actress, and her sons (Pancho's nephews and current collaborators) are the successful contemporary filmmakers Chris and Paul Weitz. Not content in the shadow of his family's accomplishments, Pancho entered the motion picture industry in Europe as an assistant to director/actor John Huston. Huston was also the star of Pancho's first film, *The Bridge in the Jungle* (1970), made in Mexico and based on a short story by B. Traven. Pancho went on to produce and direct many other feature films, including the lyrical *Mr. Sycamore* (1975), starring Jason Robards, Jean Simmons, and Sandy Dennis. Although he prefers making small, personal films, Pancho produced many of the blockbuster action pictures starring Charles Bronson, and was awarded an Emmy for producing the television series *Madeline*, based on the books by Ludwig Bemelmans. Pancho is also a writer, who adapted a screenplay for the great Swedish director Ingmar Bergman. To honor his mother on her centennial, Pancho collaborated with Lon on the coffee table book *Lupita Tovar: The Sweetheart of Mexico* (2010). Only recently, they completed Pancho's autobiography, "No Green Bananas."

Introduction

Perspective is a funny thing. Until I was writing these essays, I hadn't realized just how instrumental my father was in my becoming a film historian.

It started in the late sixties. Dad was a photographer and, as such, he spent a lot of time in camera stores and, for some reason, he always wanted me to go with him. I honestly don't know why—I made it abundantly clear that I didn't want to go. But he insisted and, well, what choice did I have? I was only eight years old—and he knew where I lived. While he was scrutinizing camera lenses for what seemed like hours, I sat on a stool at the counter, bored out of my mind. That is, until something colorful caught my eye: It was a display of small boxes containing 8mm films. Caricatures of Charlie Chaplin and Laurel & Hardy adorned the boxes on the Atlas label, and color images of Abbott & Costello and the Universal monsters were on those labeled Castle Films. They were so appealing to me that I lost track of time. Even when Dad had completed his transaction, I didn't want to leave. The next time he announced that he was headed for the camera store, I was in the car before he was. And this time, I didn't return home empty handed. Dad, always a tight man with a buck, actually handed over a five-dollar bill for four 50-foot reels, including three cartoons and a three-minute clip from a 1916 Keystone-Triangle comedy, *Fatty and Mabel Adrift*. With that one chopped-up, dupey print, I found my life's calling.

I began paying closer attention to the TV listings to see when silent films happened to be aired, which was not unusual at that time. Dad and I watched the frequently televised compilation films of independent producer Robert Youngson, beginning with *The Golden Age of Comedy* (1957). We also watched an outstanding weekly program on PBS called *The Silent Years*, hosted by Orson Welles. It marked the first time I saw such classic silents as D.W. Griffith's *Intolerance* (1916), Douglas Fairbanks's *The Mark of Zorro* (1920), Lon Chaney's *The Hunchback of Notre Dame* (1923), and Charlie Chaplin's *The Gold Rush* (1925). In those days, "old-time movies" were even shown in pizza parlors as a way to entertain customers while they were enjoying a slice. This only whetted my appetite for more—and not just pizza. I wanted to learn everything I could about the silent era—the names of the actors and directors, the titles and dates of the films, the stories behind the *making* of those films. Fortunately, Dad also enjoyed spending time at the public library, which became another of our joint destinations. He found the cinema section and picked out a volume for me: *Comedy Films, 1894-1954* (Allen & Unwin, reissued in 1968), by British author John Montgomery. This was only the beginning. I kept returning to the cinema section, seeking information from other such volumes. The late sixties and early seventies saw the release of numerous books on film, with authors like Kalton C. Lahue, Kevin Brownlow, Leonard Maltin, Anthony Slide, John McCabe, and William K. Everson coming to the fore.

My good friend Karl Keim and I hosted movie shows on balmy summer nights in my backyard, charging each of our indulgent neighbors a quarter at our makeshift box office. (In retrospect, it sounds like something the Our Gang kids would do.) Karl, an unassuming, mechanically inclined fellow, ran the projector and I handled the introductions and overall ballyhoo. I was relentless in spreading the word about silent films. My teachers encouraged me to give talks and show my films during school hours. I was even invited to be a guest speaker at neighboring high schools. Teachers found my programs to be educational; the students just thought they were fun. One especially memorable experience was being excused from a day in seventh grade to lecture at Northern Arizona University in Flagstaff. Although the students of that American History class were surprised to see a twelve-year-old standing in for their professor, they were receptive to the clips I showed and asked me numerous questions.

Before long, I outgrew the 8mm format. To show films properly in larger venues, I needed a 16mm projector. Once again, Dad came to the rescue. He and I paid a visit to a second-hand dealer who had a 1940 condensed DeVry TSI suitcase model, for which he was asking $75. Dad closed the deal for ten dollars less, making me the proud owner of that solidly built machine. Purchasing 16mm prints from Blackhawk Films and other reputable companies was an expensive proposition to be sure, but it was a necessary upgrade at that time. I then had the capacity for sound, allowing me to expand my collection to include silents with synchronized scores as well as select talkies. How I loved the texture, the suppleness, the grain, and the clarity of the wider format, especially when I had an original print to screen.

The retired movie veterans I sought out became, in some instances, close friends; others were one-time interviews. Each individual brings to mind cherished memories that have been recorded here for posterity. One friend is a comedy icon; five are authentic silent stars, and two are supporting players. Two of my other subjects are film collectors, but they are as different as two people can be. One is an Ohio-born huckster who dabbled in theatre and LGBTQ+ cinema; the other is shy, British, and an Academy Award honoree. Included also is an examination of a classic film directed by and starring Buster Keaton, and the impact his work has had on my life. And, finally, there are essays on two Los Angeles landmarks: the Motion Picture Home and Forest Lawn Memorial Park, the latter serving as an unlikely setting for a love story.

My goal, as a writer, is to avoid film book jargon and make these accounts as personal as a conversation with a friend. Although I am drawing on memories that are now in some cases fifty years old, recalling them with accuracy is not as difficult as one might imagine. I have relived those memories again and again, running them repeatedly on my internal movie projector. More than anything, I have done my best to tell my subjects' stories with honesty, humor, and compassion. Revealed herein are their triumphs and tragedies, their strengths and weaknesses, their loves and hates. It is also about human nature in general: sometimes good, sometimes not, but hopefully, always interesting.

Roll film, please.

Lon Davis

The author, at fourteen, poses for a photo to accompany a November 1973 article in the Phoenix Gazette *about the teenaged silent film collector. Photo courtesy of the Arizona State Library Archives.*

ONE

Beverly Bayne: Star of the Silent Films

Author's collection.

Nostalgia was a big business during the late sixties and early seventies, and nobody could have loved it as much as I. For me, however, it couldn't be nostalgia, since I was just a kid at the time. But everything about entertainment in the first half of the 20th century fascinated me, whether it was vaudeville, stage plays, old-time radio, vintage cartoons, films of the teens, twenties, thirties, and forties.

Capitalizing on this fascination with the past, New York City–based writer Richard Lamparski put out several volumes under the umbrella title *Whatever Became of...?* Each volume includes career overviews and then-and-now photographs of 100 formerly famous personalities. My primary interest was in those individuals who had been stars during the silent era. On pages 184-185 of Volume II, there is a career overview for Beverly Bayne. The name was familiar to me from a single entry in the Blackhawk Films catalogue, a 1914 two-reeler entitled *Under Royal Patronage*, co-starring Francis X. Bushman. His name, of course, is well known among silent film buffs because of his co-starring role as the villain Messala in *Ben-Hur: A Tale of the Christ* (1925). Bushman and Bayne were so popular with the public that they were crowned King and Queen of the Movies during "Movie Day" at the Panama-Pacific Exposition in San Diego's Balboa Park on September 11, 1915. One of the screen's first romantic duos, they were also married in real life, from 1918 to 1925. Beverly then went on to become a well-known stage actress, appearing in several Broadway shows. According to Lamparski, she was spending her retirement years in Scottsdale, Arizona, a thirty-five-minute drive from where I lived in Phoenix. I checked the telephone directory to see if Beverly Bayne was listed. She was. My parents and younger brother were enjoying an evening out on that Saturday in August 1972. I decided to take my chances and dial the number.

"Hello?"

"Is this Beverly Bayne, the silent movie star?"

"Why, yes!"

I introduced myself and told her I was thirteen and that my hobby was collecting silent films.

"Oh, my, that's wonderful!" Her voice, although textured with age, was melodic, with a dignity and clarity befitting a woman who had spent her best years on the stage. Never once during the call did she give the impression that I was impinging on her time. At one point, she told me her all-time favorite anecdote, the one involving her being discovered in 1912.

Beverly Bayne, in her early days at Essanay. Author's collection.

"I was three weeks into my freshman term at Hyde Park High School on the south side of Chicago, when a friend of mine, Grace Taylor, took me on a tour of the Essanay Film Manufacturing Company on Argyle Street. Grace's family knew Essanay's head director, Harry McRae Webster. He was very gracious, showing us the inner workings of the studio. I was entranced, for I loved everything about the theatre. We took along our photographs, because my friend said they loved to have society girls who have pretty clothes and long white gloves appear in their ballroom scenes.

"The following Tuesday afternoon, Mister Webster's secretary called after I got home from school and told me to be at the studio the following morning at ten o'clock. No sooner had I arrived than Mister Webster came rushing in with a script, which he gave to me. The title of the picture was *The Loan Shark*. He said we were to go to lunch, read the script, and that I would be playing Marion, which was the lead. Imagine, it's my first film and I had the leading role! When I was done absorbing the scenario, I was to return, and he would direct me in a scene. We did just that. He was evidently pleased with the results, for he said, 'Now little lady, you have to be here from nine in the morning until five in the afternoon each weekday, and nine until one on Saturdays.'

"The next thing he said to me was, 'So, just how much do you think you're worth?' Well, my weekly allowance was twenty-five cents, but I knew that picture people had to earn more than that! 'Umm, *thirty-five* dollars? … *Thirty*? … *Twenty-five*?' I started high and came down. He then said, 'Little lady, you will receive twenty-five dollars a week at first, and if you are selected to join the regular stock company you will receive an additional ten dollars.' My goodness, I thought, I'm going to be *rich*! And would you believe it, when I received my first paycheck, I went right out and bought myself twenty-four pairs of shoes! Can you imagine anything so silly? After I was with Essanay for six months, they raised my salary to $350 a week!"

"That's amazing!" I said. "Did the studio also hire your friend?"

"No, dear. You see, blondes did not photograph well on the film stock they were then using, and Grace was a blonde. Had she done a screen test, her hair would have registered as white, making her look like a little old lady! One of the reasons I was hired was that I had dark hair and dark eyes. Gloria Swanson, who started as an extra girl at Essanay, once sat in my dressing room and wept, saying she wished her blue eyes were brown like mine."

"Did you meet Charlie Chaplin when he was at the Chicago studio making *His New Job*?"

"Oh, yes, but it was just 'Good morning' and 'Good night' at the beginning and ending of every workday. We used to gossip behind our gloves about that funny little Englishman. He insisted that his set be obscured by screens so no one could see him working. And he would do, oh, forty or fifty takes of a scene, which was unheard of at Essanay! Why, we rarely took a scene more than once. And we were expected to complete a one-reeler in one day! Essanay really was a factory, you see. When Mister Chaplin's two-reeler reached the marketplace, it was highly praised by audiences and exhibitors alike, and it evidently was a financial success as well. This inspired our directors to take more time on each picture, instead of just cranking them out. Films not only got better, but movie acting suddenly became much less frantic. We actors were most grateful to Mister Chaplin for starting the trend."

"Do you keep in touch with other silent film actors?"

"I do! Madame Olga Petrova is a dear friend; she lives in Clearwater, Florida. From time to time I hear from Lila Lee. And then, let's see, there is Leatrice Joy, Lois Wilson, Enid Markey—oh, and not too long ago, I visited Mary Pickford and Buddy Rogers at Pickfair."

More questions and answers followed. Having kept this delightful lady on the phone for forty or so minutes, I decided to wrap up the call.

"Thank you for speaking with me," I said politely.

"The pleasure was all mine! You seem like such a nice little girl."

I was taken aback. "Actually," I said, "I'm a boy." My voice had yet to change; I was still a soprano. Miss Bayne then invited me to continue our discussion at her apartment in Scottsdale.

"I would *love* that!" I hesitated a bit before asking, "May I bring my mother along? I can't drive yet."

"Certainly. I'll look forward to meeting both of you." We agreed to a date and time, bringing an end to the first of what would be many such conversations.

My mother and I made the trip to Scottsdale, traveling through long stretches of desert landscape. We arrived at the appointed hour and were warmly greeted by our hostess. At seventy-eight, she had retained the fine features that made her one of the most photographed women in the world during the 1910s. She was, like many of her female contemporaries, small in stature, not much taller than five feet; she mentioned at one point that she wore a size four shoe. Her jet-black hair was piled high in a bun, a throwback to the Gibson Girl hairstyle of the Edwardian era, and her makeup emphasized her large expressive eyes. She and her well-trained poodle, Mitzi, occupied what was then known as an efficiency apartment, meaning that one had to be efficient to live in it, given its small size. It had a crowded look to it, with large pieces of heavy antique furniture. Clearly, she had downsized from a much larger home without purchasing new, more proportionate items. There were large mirrors on the walls, with ornate gilt frames. There was also a painting which called to mind the Mona Lisa. It turned out to be a portrait of her mother, done in the late 19th century. A reminder of more modern, less romantic times was a tall stack of yellowing issues of the *National Enquirer*. The whole place, incidentally, was redolent of moth balls.

Prior to our arrival, she had put together a tray of refreshments in her tiny kitchen. She had sliced Hostess Ho-Hos into bite-sized pieces. Fresca, a popular diet soda of that time, was the beverage of choice, over ice. I really appreciated her going to the trouble. She had also put aside some memorabilia she wished to show us, including a photo album devoted exclusively to her favorite among all her films, *Romeo and Juliet*, in which she and Francis X. Bushman starred for Metro Pictures in 1916. She proudly mentioned that she was solely responsible for the costuming choices in that sumptuous eight-reel production. She drew our attention to a still picture, featuring one costume in particular, a hooded cloak worn by Juliet.

"You know, I held onto that cloak for years," she said. "And then I was approached by a man who represented the Hollywood Museum. Someone I know went there and later described it to me as this cheap little place that charged twenty-five cents admission!"

"Miss Bayne, wasn't there—?"

"Beverly, dear."

"Beverly, wasn't there another production of *Romeo and Juliet* being made at the same time?"

"You've really done your homework, haven't you? Yes, Fox Pictures was doing one, starring Theda Bara (of all people) as Juliet! Apparently, they were hoping to change her image from that of a screen vamp to something far more innocent. William Fox, the head of the studio, had spies working for us as extras. They must have been taking notes on the way we were doing our film because when their version came out, simultaneously with ours, many of the shots, and even the subtitles, were obviously copied! The picture business was certainly different than it is today."

I nodded and took a piece of See's candy that she had kindly made available to us.

"You might find it interesting to know that we quoted every one of Shakespeare's lines faithfully. In fact, we received many letters from lip readers—deaf people—who said they had never been able to enjoy Shakespeare like that before. We were very popular with them for that." She was silent for a moment and her expression became somewhat morose. When she spoke again, there was a catch in her voice. "No prints of our film exist today. In all these years, I have avoided seeing other versions of *Romeo and Juliet*. I don't wish to spoil my memories."

Having seen *Sunset Boulevard*, Billy Wilder's 1950 film *noir* about a former silent movie queen, Norma Desmond (played by real-life former silent movie queen Gloria Swanson), I could not help but notice that Beverly shared some traits with the fictional Norma. Beverly still thought of herself as a star, decades after she had made her last film. Like most actresses, she was extremely self-centered. She told us that on a particularly important milestone birthday (her seventieth—not that she would ever admit to her real age), she had to hold the party the day before the actual date, which would have been November 22,

1963. That, tragically, was the day President John F. Kennedy was assassinated. In retrospect, Beverly fully believed that Divine Intervention had been the reason her party was pushed back to November 21. ("*God* did it," she insisted.) She also thought her fame made her a potential target of thieves and murderers. As a result, she shredded every piece of junk mail she received. If she missed even one envelope, she told me with terror in her voice, "Then some maniac would find it, see that it was addressed to a professional name, and then he would *break in and kill me*!" She was, as you surely have gathered, highly theatrical; she was also alternately charming and imperious, and given to sudden bursts of volatility. This was especially true when the topic of conversation was Francis X. Bushman.

"Mister Bushman was a vain, egotistical monster!" she said emphatically. "How I *despised* that man! In our scenes together he used every trick in the book to upstage me. From the beginning I felt that he was very insincere, and always building himself up to everybody's disadvantage. And the way he was with all the ladies on the set, flattering and kissing them—."

"Then *why* did you marry him?" I asked.

"My *dear*," she said defensively, "he threatened to *jump out of a window if I refused!* And he was so much older—almost twice my age, really. I married him with tears in my eyes."[1]

"What was it like living at Bush Manor, his estate in Maryland?"

"Well, I wasn't there any time at all, really; it was put up for auction because he couldn't make the necessary payments. Money just seemed to evaporate in that man's hands. He would rent luxury apartments when he didn't know where his next paycheck was coming from! He was terribly handsome, and he spoke beautifully, but he was so irresponsible. His eldest son later told me that he and his brothers and sisters knew that it was *I* who was sending them money each month." She paused briefly to collect her thoughts. "We were awakened one morning by the sound of loud trucks pulling onto the property. I said, 'Bushie, what *is* that?' He said, 'Oh, I thought I'd impress the neighbors by

---

1 In fact, Francis X. Bushman was ten years Beverly Bayne's senior.

Beverly Bayne and Francis X. Bushman in a scene from their serial, The Great Secret, *released in eighteen two-reel installments by Metro Pictures in 1917. Courtesy of Kevin Brownlow.*

To support herself and her son during her husband's year-long absence, Beverly Bayne starred in five features. This is a publicity shot for The Age of Innocence *(1924). Author's collection.*

having all the trees fixed.' Honestly! So I said, 'And *how* exactly are we going to *pay* for that?' and he said, 'I'm sure you'll think of a way, Bev.'" With that, she banged her fist loudly on the wooden arm of her chair.

She went on to explain that he had been offered a role in *Ben-Hur*, which was originally to be shot on location in Rome. Beverly had no interest in accompanying him as she found Rome to be a noxious, dirty city. Francis sailed for Italy, alone. Because that production was fraught with workers' strikes and delays, he remained in Europe for more than a year. Beverly, meanwhile, starred in several films: *The Age of Innocence*, *The Tenth Woman*, *Her Marriage Vow* (all for Warner Bros., 1924), *Who Cares* (Columbia, 1925), and *Passionate Youth* (Truart, also 1925). This marked the end of her career as a movie actress; from then on she worked solely on the stage, whether it was on the Keith-Orpheum vaudeville circuit, on Broadway, or in stock. Her marriage also came to an end. She informed the press of her separation from Francis X. Bushman in January 1925, and was awarded a divorce in April of that year. The only good thing that had come out of that marriage, she told us, was their son, Richard, who was born in 1919. She mentioned that he had passed away five years earlier, but she refrained from going into any detail.

Sensing her discomfort, I changed the subject back to her career. Would she ever entertain the idea of making a comeback? She shook her head.

"No, dear. My final curtain call took place in 1958. When The Sombrero Playhouse in Phoenix did its production of Rose Franken's *Claudia*, I accepted the role I had performed in the Chicago touring company, that of Mrs. Brown, the lead character's mother. To me, it felt like the perfect way to end my career. You know, dear, the little theatres are the only hope we have of keeping the performing arts alive in this country. The great producers are gone. With the costs of production being what they are, professional theatre is so limited that the community players have a significance it's never had before." She also touched on her activism. A proud citizen of Scottsdale, she wrote frequent letters to

Beverly Bayne as she appeared in the Chicago touring company of Rose Franken's Claudia, *in 1941.*

the editor of the local newspaper, championing the concept of keeping "the West's most Western town" the small city it was. Politically, she was an ultra-conservative Republican, not unlike several of her silent film contemporaries (e.g., Gloria Swanson, Colleen Moore, Patsy Ruth Miller, Harold Lloyd). It almost makes one wonder if the Hollywood of the twenties roared as loudly as some have claimed. But then, there is often a major difference in someone's attitudes in their twenties versus their seventies.

Another of her pet subjects was the degeneration of entertainment in America, particularly in the motion picture industry. X-rated films had temporarily gone mainstream: *Myra Breckinridge*, *Carnal Knowledge*, and *Midnight Cowboy* were then playing at the nation's movie theatres. She condemned this trend, saying, "I don't wish to sully my mind." Beverly, in fairness, was also quick to mention a couple of recent films she had seen and enjoyed: *Nicholas and Alexandra* (1971), a dramatization of the fall of the Russian aristocracy, and *Patton* (1970), starring George C. Scott as the tough-as-nails World War II four-star general. She also loved the James Bond movies and network television shows such as *Cannon*, with William Conrad as a corpulent detective, and *Barnaby Jones*, starring Buddy Ebsen as a geriatric detective.

After two spirited hours of non-stop conversation, my mother suggested we take our leave. Kisses and hugs were exchanged and promises of future visits were made. Beverly gifted me with her personal hardback copy of the *Whatever Became of ...?* book that had led me to her in the first place. In her flamboyant handwriting, she inscribed the title page, "To my best 'silent picture fan,' Aim high! Fondly, Beverly Bayne." My mother asked for an autograph for her seventy-five-year-old mother, who remembered Bushman and Bayne from her youth. On a piece of scratch paper, she wrote, "To Ann Gallagher, Lest we forget," below which she signed her name. Beverly also loaned me her first edition, signed copy of Lillian Gish's recently published biography, *The Movies, Mr. Griffith, and Me* (Prentice-Hall, 1969).

Opening the front door, her already large eyes widened in horror. The splayed fingers on her right hand were held in mid-air over her frightened visage; it was a gesture that could only be made by a heroine in a silent movie melodrama. And what, pray tell, was the cause of this histrionic display? A major dust storm was quickly approaching! As a sixteen-year resident of the Valley of the Sun, Beverly warned us not to chance a drive home until it passed. But because this was our first exposure to that meteorological phenomenon (also known as a *haboob*), we foolishly thought we could manage it. Think again. The air was so thick with dust and dirt that visibility quickly dropped to 0 miles. We were incredibly thankful to make it home alive.

Later that day, my mother told me about a startling discovery she made during our visit. At one point, Beverly handed her a prized possession, her family Bible, in which she kept numerous inspirational passages. As Mom was looking through it, she happened upon a newspaper obituary, which read, "Richard S. Bayne, 47; a Suicide." She quickly closed the book. Only later did I learn the tragic details from a variety of sources, including Wallace Beery's daughter, Carol Ann, a close friend of the Bayne family. Beverly, it seems, controlled every aspect of her son's life. In 1941, the year he graduated from Rutgers University, Richard legally changed his last name from Bushman to Bayne. Intelligent and well-mannered, he was expected to act as the attentive escort to his social butterfly mother.

Richard grew to be a tall, handsome man, somewhat along the lines of Tyrone Power. Despite his movie star looks, he determined early on that he did not wish to follow in his parents' footsteps by becoming an actor; the business was simply too erratic. He chose instead to live a quiet existence, working as a floorwalker at Goldwater's newly opened department store in Phoenix. His anonymity was upset in June 1957 when Joe Hyams, a syndicated columnist for the *New York Herald Tribune*, broke a story with the headline, "Ex-Star Pines for Lost Son." The columnist gave the distinct impression that seventy-five-year-old Francis X. Bushman was heartbroken over the lack of contact with his youngest child. Bushman was quoted as saying that Beverly had gone against a judge's orders and taken their four-year-old son to New York, never to return to California. He also said that it was a son's responsibility to reach out to his father. Beverly was incensed by the column. Richard, however, gave a measured statement to the press, claiming that he would very much like to speak with him. No such meeting ever took place. When I asked Bushman's widow, Iva, about this item, she claimed that Hyams had distorted her late husband's statement. According to her, Francis had only wanted to say hello to Richard "once every four or five years." He also expressed surprise that his son had never married. After all, he reasoned, "any son of Bushman should be a real *he-man*."

If Richard was avoiding marriage it was because his mother believed that her grown son should remain single until after her death. The inevitable clash between the two occurred in the mid-sixties when Richard met the woman he wished to marry. Iva Bushman privately told me that the woman in question paid her husband a visit at his home in Pacific Palisades, California. She tearfully explained that Beverly had been feigning heart attacks to manipulate Richard into staying with her. Francis gently told her that he had no influence over his son—or over Beverly.

Francis X. Bushman died at the age of eighty-three on August 23, 1966. On February 4, 1967, Richard was at home, alone. He went into the bathroom, carrying a handgun. Putting the muzzle of the firearm to his temple, he pulled the trigger. Beverly found his body later that day. She tried desperately to suppress that horrific memory by never, ever discussing it. If pressed, Beverly would say that Richard had died as the result of a traffic accident in front of their apartment building.

Beverly received significant recognition for her contribution to early American cinema. She was among the first actors to have a star on the Hollywood Walk of Fame (located at 1770 Vine Street, in front of the Capitol Records Tower). On January 14, 1971, she made an appearance on "A Special Salute to the Silent Screen" episode of *The Merv Griffin Show*, along with several other former stars. A Chicago filmmaker was putting together a documentary about Beverly's life. She was also the subject of flattering articles in both local and national magazines and newspapers. Just days after our first visit, The Cinephiles Society, a group of silent film aficionados, flew Beverly to Washington, D.C., where she, Lois Wilson, and Leatrice Joy were honored at a well-publicized ceremony during Cinecon 8. Beverly's contribution to the evening was an elegant reading of the balcony soliloquy from *Romeo and Juliet*, Act II, Scene II. She relished reciting this familiar passage whenever the mood struck her: "O Romeo, Romeo! Wherefore art thou, Romeo?"

The entire trip to Washington, D.C., was a major highlight of Beverly's retirement years. I was flattered that she took the time during those eventful few days to send me an enthusiastically written postcard. As she told the *Phoenix Gazette* upon her return home: "I don't mind telling you that they gave me a standing ovation. It was quite a thrill.... It proved there's life in the old girl yet.... For four days my hotel suite was hardly bare of people who wanted to visit." To another newspaper reporter, she said, "I take this renewed interest [in my film career] with gratitude. One of the things I tried to do in my acting was to make people happy. I find it marvelous that, after all these years, they still find happiness in my work."

I was determined to add my own heartfelt tribute to the mix. My idea was to co-host a screening of two Beverly Bayne films, with the star in attendance. The screening would take place at the Phoenix home of my friend Gary Lacher. Gary, a thirty-three-year-old news photographer, had transformed the ordinary living room of his ordinary tract house into an extraordinary home theatre, when such a luxury was usually reserved for movie moguls. Adjoining the living room was a small bedroom that had been outfitted as a projection booth, containing two 35mm projectors and a 16mm model. A narrow glass-covered window was professionally cut into the wall facing a screen at the far end of the living room. It was covered by a theatre-style curtain, which parted at the press of a button.

Beverly must have had her fill of tributes because, when I broached the topic, her response was tepid at best; what's more, it did not improve in subsequent conversations. But being young, stubborn, and dumb as a rock, I did not heed her implied objections. I barreled ahead, finally getting her to agree to a screening, which was scheduled for the evening of Friday, December 21, 1973.

The first order of business was acquiring the needed films. With my father's assistance, I wrote a letter to the American Film Institute in Washington, D.C., to inquire about a Beverly Bayne short subject in their vast collection. It was *Teaching Hickville to Sing*, an Essanay one-reel comedy from 1913. A slight work, it is significant for being one of only a few surviving prints of the hundreds of films she made. The other title I planned to show was the previously mentioned *Under Royal Patronage*. Once we had the prints in hand, Gary and I made a trip to the home of seventy-three-year-old Roberta Bragdon, an authentic silent movie accompanist. (I had only recently met Gary and Roberta at a showing of *Broken Blossoms* at Arizona State University in Tempe.) I lugged my projector into Roberta's music room, and Gary brought in his clunky reel-to-reel tape recorder. After viewing both films in silence, Roberta did a marvelous job, playing the organ in time with the action. These recordings would be played during the screening.

After weeks of planning, the big night was finally here! The guests began arriving at the designated hour. My mother, father, sister, and brother were all there, as were Roberta Bragdon and her brother Paul. A handful of cinema students from ASU showed up, as did their distinguished, grey-bearded professor, who hosted a Saturday night classic film program on the local PBS affiliate. Hoping to turn the evening into an historic event, I had even invited a reporter from the *Arizona Republic*. He never showed, much to my later relief. The only other no-show was the guest of honor.

I went into Gary's office, closed the door, and dialed Beverly's phone number. No answer. Already a nervous wreck, I became positively anxiety ridden. Because Beverly had driven to my house in her bright yellow Ford Mustang the previous autumn, I assumed she would have no trouble finding the current location.

Of course, she made that other drive in the daytime, and seniors often avoid driving at night. Taking my father aside, I told him I was unable to reach Beverly, and that I was concerned for her safety. He and my mother immediately drove to her apartment to investigate. What they found was Beverly in her nightgown, lying face up on the floor of her bedroom; she was heavily intoxicated. Perhaps they should have assisted her into her bed and left her there, but they chose instead to help her get ready to be fêted. My mother had the unenviable task of getting poor Beverly out of her nightgown and into a dress. And then, because Beverly's hair—which had turned grey since the last time I had seen her—was unkempt, my mother attempted to style it. Beverly grew impatient with her tentative efforts. "SPRAAAAAAAAAY!" she admonished, pushing a can of hairspray into my mother's hand. After spraaaaaaaying her hair to a fare-thee-well, she did a rather inexact job of applying Beverly's fuchsia-colored lipstick. While this was going on, my father called me. He mentioned my friend's delicate condition, adding that Beverly should no longer live alone.

When my parents, with Beverly in tow, showed up at the front door, I knew immediately that my troubles were far from over. Beverly was obviously still in her cups. I assisted her over to a davenport located just below the projector's light beam. Gary, a seasoned host of innumerable screenings, had taken it upon himself to run a few of his short silent films, including one by surrealist Georges Méliès—as if this evening wasn't surreal enough already. Despite her condition—or perhaps because of it—Beverly was in high spirits. Seated next to her was my good-natured eleven-year-old brother, Chris. He was the object of Beverly's affection that night. She held onto him tightly and smothered him with endless whiskey-scented kisses. "You won't forget me, will you, dear?" she asked him again and again. Gary had threaded up the first film, the indifferent *Hickville* comedy, in which the nineteen-year-old Beverly portrays an actress stranded in a bucolic village. To earn her keep, she opens a music school for the town's half-witted citizens. Roberta's music score markedly enhanced the presentation.

The main feature was up next. Based on a short story by George Barr McCutcheon, the two-reel drama *Under Royal Patronage* tells the tale of a Ruritanian prince and princess who temporarily trade places with two commoners. A critic for *Moving Picture World* stated, "Miss Bayne is altogether lovely as the Princess. There is an unaffected sweetness in her impersonation that fits the part admirably." The two-reeler was so popular at the time of its original release that it was reissued two years later. Unfortunately, it did not prove to be the best selection for the present occasion. Shortly into reel one, there he was, bigger than life—that vain, egotistical monster Francis X. Bushman!

"BOOOOOOOOOOOO!" Beverly yelled. She encouraged Chris to boo along with her every time her former leading man appeared onscreen. Other members of the audience soon joined in. All I could think was how grateful I was that the reporter had failed to show.

Afterward, the lights came on and the professor weighed in on the films, particularly concerning Beverly's performances. I believe "charming" was the predicate adjective he used. It turns out that this erudite gentleman also fancied himself a caricaturist. He had been doodling on his artist's pad since Beverly's arrival. And, indeed, he captured her likeness, perhaps too well. Every wrinkle, both chins, and her rat's-nest hairdo were on the page in unforgiving detail.

Please don't show it to her, please don't show it to her, I said prayerfully to myself.

He showed it to her.

"Is that supposed to be *me*?" she said with mock horror. "Why, I look nine hundred and ninety-nine thousand years old!"

The artist then inveigled her into autographing the unflattering drawing.

The following morning, I gave Beverly a call, waiting until "after eleven," as she always specified. She sounded completely sober and not in the least hungover. I was waiting to see if she said anything at all about the previous evening, but she did not. That is, not until the moment she was about to hang up. "Oh, and dear," she said, almost as an afterthought, "thank you for the lovely party."

From that point forward, Beverly gradually lost her independence. Someone with the power of attorney (I don't know who) insisted that the newly minted octogenarian surrender her sweet little dog and move out of her apartment. Her belongings went into storage, and Beverly was installed in a procession of nursing facilities. After living on her own since her son's death seven years earlier, she did not take well to this affront to her lifestyle. She called various admirers, including my fourteen-year-old self, to sneak in a bottle of whiskey for her. When refused, she became hostile. I visited her in a number of these sterile places. Pausing briefly at the partially open door of her room, I saw Beverly lying on a regulation hospital bed, a forlorn expression on her weathered face. When I knocked, she quickly grabbed a large pink bow, stuck it in her hair, and sat up ramrod straight. With an imperious gesture, she announced, "COME!" Throughout our brief visit, she was utterly gracious, with no reference to the missing whiskey bottle.

In 1974, my family and I moved to San Diego County. I kept in touch with Beverly, but the news was never good; she was dreadfully unhappy with her living situation, regardless of where that was. At my behest, character actor Iggie Wolfington arranged to have Beverly become a patient of the Motion Picture and Television Country House and Hospital in Woodland Hills, California. My great uncle, Ted Edlin, a fifty-year member of the Screen Extras Guild, spent his final years at the facility's hospital and always praised the staff, the food, and the campus's peaceful setting. It was my fervent hope that the Home's top-notch medical staff could treat Beverly's alcoholism. Several weeks after she had been admitted, I visited her during the holiday season of 1975. Never had I seen her in such an agitated state. She *hated*

Beverly paid a visit to Lon's family's home in Phoenix in October 1972. Photo by Paul G. Blabac.

living at the Home, she said; it was filled with "old people and cripples." In addition, she missed Scottsdale. Before long, her wish to return there was granted.

Around this time, Grace Randall stepped assuredly into the rapidly deteriorating situation. Grace, a mature woman of means, became Beverly's constant companion and benefactress. The recuperative effect that Grace had on her was remarkable. Beverly began wearing makeup and dressing well again. She also dwelt less on Bushman; in fact, she told one interviewer that she would no longer answer questions about him.

On one of my infrequent trips to Arizona, I visited Beverly at The Beatitudes Campus. A brochure for this lovely place describes it as "a not-for-profit life-plan community founded in 1965 by the Church of the Beatitudes." Grace encouraged Beverly to stroll with her around the facility's beautifully maintained grounds with its colorful flower beds. Just prior to my leaving,

Beverly took my hand in hers. I could feel a piece of paper cross my palm. Money! I looked at her as if to say, "Oh, I couldn't possibly—," when she said, with fire in those ever-expressive eyes, "I'll break it," referring to my hand. It was a crisp twenty-dollar bill. I deeply appreciated that sweet, grandmotherly gesture.

The last time I saw Beverly she had suffered a stroke and could no longer speak but for a few words. It was heartbreaking to see her like this, but I kept a smile on my face and showed her several of the still pictures she had given me over the years. The one that especially caught her attention was the striking portrait she had signed for me on our first in-person visit. "That's *lovely!*" she managed to say. It was as though she were looking at someone other than herself. I leaned over and kissed her on the cheek.

Beverly Pearl Bayne died peacefully on August 28, 1982; she was eighty-eight years old. Grace Randall, bless her heart, purchased a Laurentian Rose Rock of Ages granite marker for Beverly's grave in the Paradise Memorial Gardens, located in her beloved Scottsdale. The stone is adorned with a floral spray to the left of her name, the masks of comedy and tragedy below, with the legend "Star of the Silent Films" inscribed for all time.

TWO

The Motion Picture and Television Fund: There's No Place Like the Home

There is a wonderful home for motion picture veterans in Hollywood–private, luxurious, out of reach of sightseers–yet I know of several old-timers who, on being urged to retire to its spacious grounds, have preferred to live on in loneliness in little rooms, keeping their independence to the last.

Joe Franklin,
Classics of the Silent Screen, 1959

Photo courtesy of Marc Wanamaker, Bison Archives.

During the 1930s, more than a few silent stars came to tragic ends. The list includes Roscoe "Fatty" Arbuckle, once Chaplin's only rival, who died virtually broke in his forties. John Gilbert, the great matinee idol whose career was supposedly destroyed by the talkies, essentially drank himself to death at age thirty-eight. Someone with the same sad fate was the once-vivacious Mack Sennett Bathing Beauty Marie Prevost. Karl Dane, the goofy-looking Danish actor best known for his comedy roles, and Florence Lawrence, the Biograph Girl, who held that title prior to Mary Pickford, were so discouraged by their unemployment that they took their own lives. With casualties mounting, something had to be done, and quickly, for those industry members facing hard times.

In 1939, another Dutch actor, Jean Hersholt, was the president of the Motion Picture Relief Fund (later known as the Motion Picture and Television Fund, or MPTF), which had been created by Mary Pickford in 1921. The two philanthropists were considering an idea that would provide needed medical care and a comfortable place to live for those whose careers were behind them. Hersholt discovered a large parcel of land, forty-one acres, for sale in the San Fernando Valley. Reasonably priced at $850 an acre, the property was populated by walnut and orange groves. Hersholt, the namesake of the Academy's Humanitarian Award, encouraged the fund's board members to purchase the land and begin building. Since 1942, the Motion Picture Country House and Hospital, located at 23388 Mulholland Drive in Woodland

Hills, has been an oasis for those who are elderly, ill, or financially insecure. Those with money are expected to pay their way; those without money pay nothing. There is a state-of-the-art hospital with nearly two hundred beds; a country house; sixty cottage apartments; and the lodge, with its sixty furnished rooms, for residents in need of a higher level of care. The complex also has its own barbershop, beauty salon, movie theatre, and chapel, all on well-maintained grounds. The fund's motto is "We take care of our own."

Ted Edlin (left) seems concerned about something in For Heaven's Sake (1926), starring Harold Lloyd (center). Photo courtesy of Steve Massa.

The author, age twelve, meets his seventy-six-year-old great-uncle Ted Edlin in the lobby of the Motion Picture Hospital on November 26, 1971. Photo by Paul G. Blabac.

My initial visit to the Motion Picture Home occurred on November 26, 1971. It was a stop my family made on the long drive home to Phoenix, Arizona, from Northern California's Bay Area, where we spent the Thanksgiving holiday with my father's sister Irene and her husband, Alvin. During a stop in Los Angeles, we paid a visit to Alvin's uncle Theodore Maxwell Edlin.

Born in San Francisco on October 3, 1894, he was a boy of talent and drive. He became a published songwriter at sixteen, writing "That Lovable Ragtime" and "My Dear Girl." He also wrote many vaudeville sketches and monologues. With Del St. Lawrence, he co-wrote four two-reel dramas that were produced by Liberty Films, the first movie studio located in San Mateo. Ted Edlin's career as an actor began promisingly in 1915 with two features: *Love Finds a Way* and *The Peacemaker*. But the fates decided that stardom would never be his. Instead, he found himself in film after film, without billing.

A regular in Harold Lloyd's silent features, Ted appears as a young romantic, and later as a wedding guest, in *Girl Shy* (1924), and in *For Heaven's Sake* (1926), he is one of Harold's cronies, trying desperately to save him from matrimony. Ted even has his own intertitle in that one, which is a line more than all the dialogue he had in the sound era.

Extras of that time were expected to provide their own wardrobes. This meant they had to have appropriate suits, hats, and the requisite evening clothes. Thus attired, they usually spent their working hours awaiting the next setup in the broiling California sun. If this brought hardship, Ted didn't mention it. He was just grateful for the chance to work, whether in a low-budget two-reel comedy or an A-picture on one of the bigger lots. Attempting to earn a living on an extra's salary was not easy. That may explain his motivation behind learning the craft of makeup. During World War II, he was at 20th Century-Fox, applying powder and rouge to the gorgeous faces of such starlets as Linda Darnell and Rita Hayworth. One of the productions he was known to have worked on was the 1945 film *A Medal for Benny*, starring Dorothy Lamour and Academy Award nominee J. Carrol Naish.

But being an actor—even an unrecognized one—has a way of getting into a person's blood. Every other occupation seems almost bland by comparison. So, he continued to show up at casting calls, hoping for that one big break.

Age proved to be a great benefit to him as his immaculately groomed white hair and mustache gave him the distinguished look needed by casting directors. He is a patron at the nightclub featuring "The Bowery Thrush" in *Blues Busters* (1950); a prominent audience member in *Mr. Music* (also 1950), attentively watching Bing Crosby and Groucho Marx perform a song-and-dance number; a distressed partygoer in a climactic scene in *Some Like it Hot* (1959); a pedestrian sharing a few frames with Doris Day in *Midnight Lace* (1960); a parsimonious elder statesman in *Mary Poppins* (1964); a tuxedo-clad millionaire looking down his aristocratic nose at the common, but unsinkable, Molly Brown (Debbie Reynolds), in that 1964 musical; yet another theatregoer, this time seated next to Florenz Ziegfeld (Walter Pidgeon) in the 1968 Fanny Brice biopic *Funny Girl*; and in what must have been one of his last jobs, an enthusiastic admirer of Mae West during her musical number in *Myra Breckinridge* (1970). There were, of course, countless other such brief appearances in his fifty years as a member of the Screen Extras Guild (SEG).

When his health began to fail, the now-retired seventy-six-year-old became a permanent resident of the Motion Picture Hospital. Getting to know him through our written correspondence, I found him to be a sweet, gentle man, one who deeply appreciated a member of his family taking the time to write to him. He was pleased when I mentioned that my parents, brother, and sister would be stopping in to see him the day after Thanksgiving.

While waiting in the hospital lobby for Uncle Ted to arrive, I went up to the reception desk and asked who some of the notable residents were. I was told, nicely but firmly, that such information was strictly confidential. This was frustrating to me, of course. I imagined that some of my favorite silent film actors were there, just waiting to share their histories with a receptive listener. As I was contemplating this, Uncle Ted arrived in the lobby. He looked just like his most recent head shot, although he had clearly lost a significant amount of weight in the past year. I walked over to him, and we wordlessly gave each other a hug and a kiss. We joined my family in a sitting area and had a nice chat. In gratitude for my cards and letters, he kindly presented me with a box of licorice nips that he purchased in the hospital's gift shop.

A stop at the Motion Picture Home became a regular part of our Thanksgiving trip for the next few years. I would be dropped off at the entrance as the rest of my family went to dinner. Meanwhile, I dined with Uncle Ted in the facility's cafeteria. I always did my best to cheer him up, but it wasn't easy. A depressive, Ted would not reveal what was saddening him so. Dementia had also robbed him of his memories, leaving him with little-to-no recollections of his fifty-year career in movies. This made conversation a challenge. If I asked how he was feeling, he would say, "Terrible." Five minutes later, I'd ask him again, only to hear: "Worse." Invariably, after dinner, he would nod off. That was my cue to roam the halls of the hospital, greeting patients who happened by. My first question was always, "What did you do in the movie business?" One man I talked with was an accomplished stills photographer. One no-nonsense lady was Louis B. Mayer's secretary, perhaps one of many. An outgoing gentleman enthusiastically told me he had been one of the Wicked Witch's guards in *The Wizard of Oz* (1939). These still-vital men and women were not stars, but in their own ways they contributed to the evolving industry. I gradually learned who some of the better-known inhabitants were.

- Donald Crisp, the former silent film actor and director, who won a Best Supporting Oscar for his sensitive portrayal of the father in *How Green Was My Valley* (1941).
- Betty Blythe, who played the title role in the 1921 epic *The Queen of Sheba*.
- G. M. "Broncho Billy" Anderson, the pioneering western star of *The Great Train Robbery* (1903), and the co-founder

(with George K. Spoor) of the Essanay Film Manufacturing Company.
- Otto Kruger, the distinguished character actor who was so memorable as the pragmatic judge in *High Noon* (1952).
- Louella Parsons, one of Hollywood's first gossip columnists. The biggest stars bowed down to her and showered her with elaborate gifts to assure they were treated well in her influential column.
- Dorothy Davenport, a filmmaker who had been married to silent screen idol Wallace Reid. In 1923, the thirty-one-year-old Reid was seriously injured while on location. He died tragically following a morphine overdose. Davenport later spoke out on the dangers of narcotics addiction.
- Minta Durfee, the Keystone actress who was Charlie Chaplin's first onscreen leading lady. The first wife of Roscoe Arbuckle, Minta stood faithfully by her husband during and after the infamous 1921–1922 trials in which he was tried for rape and manslaughter. He was found innocent of all charges, but his career had been destroyed in the process. Addie McPhail, Arbuckle's third wife, was a volunteer nurse at the Motion Picture Home for seventeen years. The two ladies got along surprisingly well.
- Bud Abbott, of Abbott and Costello, had suffered a series of strokes since his partner's death in 1959 and was at the Home on an out-patient basis.
- Jerry Colonna, the mustachioed comedian from Bob Hope's radio program. Like Bud Abbott, he was at the Home temporarily to receive physical therapy following a stroke.
- Blossom Rock (Marie Blake), the actress who found fame with her final role, that of Grandmama on ABC-TV's *The Addams Family*.
- Mitchell Leisen, the director of *Death Takes a Holiday* (1934).
- Bess Flowers, known as "Queen of the Dress Extras."

- Allyn Joslyn, a nonconformist actor known for his roles on Broadway, in films, and on television. While undergoing a routine medical procedure, something went awry, causing him to lose the ability to walk for the remaining ten years of his life.
- Mary Astor, a former silent film actress who later played the femme fatale in *The Maltese Falcon* (1941), starring Humphrey Bogart as Private Eye Sam Spade.
- Jean Hagen, the brilliant comic actress who played the screechy-voiced silent film star Lina Lamont in MGM's musical comedy *Singin' in the Rain* (1952).

Some of the residents, like Louella Parsons and G. M. Anderson, were dealing with dementia and had been moved to a different location. Others, like Otto Kruger, were too ill to receive visitors. Mary Astor lived independently in one of the cottages but made it clear that she preferred her own company to anyone else's. And a few—like Jean Hagen, Minta Durfee, Blossom Rock, and Bess Flowers—enjoyed communicating with other residents and the occasional visitor. Fortunately, that welcoming group also included Larry Fine of The Three Stooges.

He was born Louis Feinberg at 606 South Third Street in Philadelphia, Pennsylvania, on October 5, 1902. As a toddler, he sustained an injury that would indirectly lead to his career in show business. His father was looking after him one day as he addressed some projects in his watch repair and jewelry shop. While his back was turned, his infant son reached for the bottle of acid used to evaluate gold. Before the child could drink from it, he knocked the bottle out of his hand, inadvertently spilling acid on the baby's arm. The burn was severe and required a skin graft. Doctors feared that it would even impede his growth. It was therefore recommended that he take violin lessons as soon as possible, since the action of moving the bow back and forth might strengthen his arm and hand muscles. The boy did as he was told and developed a life-long love of music.

Larry Fine publicity shot, Columbia Pictures, 1946, taken from the original camera negative. Courtesy of Scott H. Reboul.

Truth to tell, he was not an especially gifted musician, but what talent he did possess allowed him to find steady work in small-time vaudeville, beginning at the age of thirteen. Changing his name to Larry Fine (a shorter name meant bigger letters on the marquee), he developed an act he called "At the Crossroads," featuring the singing Haney Sisters. They toured the RKO, Orpheum, Keith-Orpheum, and Delmar vaudeville circuits between 1921 and 1925. The Haney Sisters and Fine eventually dissolved the act, but Larry's personal relationship with Mabel Haney flourished. They were in love, and not even their differing religions (he was Jewish; she was Roman Catholic) could keep them apart. In 1926, Larry and Mabel were married. They had two children, a daughter named Phyllis and a boy named Johnny.

Roughhouse comedian Ted Healy, along with his sidekicks, brothers Moe and Shemp Howard, saw the bushy-haired Larry in 1928 at Chicago's Rainbo Gardens nightclub and felt he would make a good addition to their act. Moe later said that he and Ted approached Larry backstage and offered him the job—provided he left the violin at home. Larry agreed. Playing only the best theatres, Ted Healy and His Stooges eventually went to Hollywood and starred in their first feature, *Soup to Nuts* (1930), written by Rube Goldberg. In 1932, Shemp left the act to pursue a solo movie career and was replaced by his younger brother Jerome, known as Curly. Healy, Howard, Fine, and Howard worked for a time at MGM, appearing in such features as *Dancing Lady* (1933), starring Clark Gable, Joan Crawford, and a little-known tap dancer named Fred Astaire. Healy and the Boys also made a series of five two-reelers, three of which are in two-color Technicolor.

Moe, Larry, and Curly broke free of Healy and formed their own act, The Three Stooges. Jules White, who oversaw the short subjects department of Columbia Pictures on Gower Street, hired them to star in their own series of two-reelers, beginning in 1934. They would go on to make 190 shorts for the studio in the subsequent twenty-four years. These twenty-minute comedy farces were so popular with the public that they were often a bigger draw than the program's main feature. This is understandable. Timeless in nature, the better shorts are as fresh and funny today as they were on their initial release. The indelible characters of the Stooges have become a treasured part of American folklore. Moe is the bullying leader, Larry is the eternal middleman, and Curly is a bizarre man-child given to odd quirks and weird noises. Whether posing as plumbers, exterminators, chefs, or decorators, these three ruffians create chaos wherever they go. With very little effort, they can destroy any high society soirée with their pie-throwing and general incompetence. This "upsetting of dignity"—Moe's succinct phrase—greatly appealed to Depression-era audiences, just as it appeals to contemporary viewers.

Storylines for the shorts were often determined by set availability. If there was a medieval castle erected for a feature, the Stooges would no doubt be playing knights; if there was a western saloon, they would be cowboys; if there was a gothic mansion, they would be paying a visit to a haunted house, and so on and so forth. Not only were the sets hand-me-downs, but so were many of the gags. Stooge shorts, particularly those featuring Curly, are rife with routines that had been done in the silent era. I'm referring to the live oyster in the soup bit, mistaking a balloon with a hat for an intruder, carrying blocks of ice up a ridiculously long flight of stairs. These and other set pieces—not to mention a heavy reliance on custard pies—were adroitly handled by Moe and company. The reason for this is basic: Del Lord, one of the Stooges' best and most influential directors, and writers Clyde Bruckman, Felix Adler, and Ewart Adamson had all worked for Mack Sennett in the twenties.

In 1946, forty-two-year-old Curly Howard was felled by a stroke during the filming of the team's ninety-seventh short. Forced to retire from acting, he died in 1952. Brother Shemp rejoined the act in 1947. Another inspired comic-actor, Shemp was an inveterate wisecracker, hiding his cowardly nature behind a tough-guy veneer. He appeared in seventy-seven Stooge shorts, the final four of which were produced posthumously in 1956, courtesy of stock footage and the use of a double. To complete the remaining sixteen shorts, Moe and Larry worked with fellow contract player Joe Besser, whose character was that of a middle-aged sissy. This marked the nadir of the Stooges' career. Two-reelers were considered hopelessly old-fashioned. Budget cuts reduced the shorts' running time to fifteen minutes, and many were scene-for-scene remakes of earlier titles, relying heavily on stock footage. On the last day of December 1957, Columbia closed its shorts department. The Stooges were officially out of a job, with no solid prospects on the horizon.

Miraculously, they would reach unprecedented heights when their old comedies (with Curly) began turning up on television, making a new generation of fans, particularly boys twelve and under. Although Moe and Larry did not receive a cent in residuals from these showings, they found themselves in demand once again. They hired a new Third Stooge, a roly-poly vaudeville and burlesque comic named Joe DeRita, whom they dubbed Curly-Joe. The team, guided by Moe's son-in-law Norman Maurer, toned down the heavy use of slapstick by retiring, among other bits, the easily imitable two-fingered eye-poke. These kinder, gentler Stooges starred in some family-friendly features, a cartoon series, and toured extensively in their hugely successful stage show. They also endorsed a plethora of novelty items bearing their likenesses—everything from comic books to trading cards to Halloween masks. There were also television commercials for Hot Shot insecticide, Aqua Net hairspray, Metropolitan Life Insurance, Chunky Chocolates, and Instant Simoniz car wax. More than ever, the Stooges were also traveling philanthropists, making numerous, unpublicized visits to orphanages and children's hospitals, always arriving on Christmas morning with a carload of presents.

The Three Stooges lasted longer than any other classic comedy team, making television guest appearances until the late sixties. Ironically, that was when this nine-year-old boy first became aware of them. My family and I were watching ABC-TV's *Wide World of Sports* ("The thrill of victory! The agony of defeat!") on March 31, 1969, when the Stooges' commercial for Williamson-Dickie Manufacturing Company made its network debut. In the sixty-second color film (although we still had a black-and-white set), Moe, Larry, and Curly-Joe wreak havoc at a construction site. Among other indignities, they are buried in a shower of bricks and land in wet cement. "But don't worry," announcer Russell Arms says, "they're wearing Dickie work clothes." Now cleaned up and smiling, the Stooges stand in the background as

This composite shot represents The Four Stages of The Three Stooges. Upper left: the Curly era, which lasted from 1932 to 1946; Upper right: the Shemp years, 1947 to 1955; lower left: the Joe Besser interval of 1956-1957; and bottom right: the golden years, with Curly-Joe, from 1958 to 1970.

Arms (on camera) adds, "If Dickies can make *The Three Stooges* look good, imagine how great *you'll* look!" At that moment, he is smacked in the face with a pie.

When I enthusiastically described this commercial to my neighbor Timmy Shattuck, he invited me to join a group of boys who watched the Stooges each weekday afternoon on New York

City's WPIX, Channel 11. The lineup of shows scheduled from three thirty to six o'clock was just made for the station's twelve-and-under-male demographic.

3:30 SPEED RACER—Cartoon
4:00 ABBOTT AND COSTELLO—Comedy
4:30 THREE STOOGES—Comedy
5:00 SUPERMAN—Adventure
5:30 MUNSTERS—Comedy

The genial host of *The Three Stooges Show* was Joe Bolton, a one-time TV weatherman who wore a police uniform and called himself "Officer Joe." Exactly which "Third Stooge" would be featured depended on the day of the week. Mondays and Thursdays were reserved for the ever-popular Curly; Tuesdays and Fridays were for Shemp; and Joe Besser was relegated to Wednesdays. Watching those films with our usual group made the experience all the more hilarious. There were times when I laughed so hard I was in danger of wetting my pants. The Stooges' more extreme slapstick, particularly in those shorts directed by Jules White, was exciting to watch. It provided something like the sensation an average teenager must experience when listening to hard-rock music. Moe was a master at hitting, slapping, and eye-poking. He was equally adept at misusing various tools, like hammers, saws, pliers, wrenches, and lead pipes on his hapless subordinates. Cartoonish sound effects provided an essential comedic element to these assaults. When Moe slaps Larry, the sound of a whiplash accentuates the action. If he pokes Shemp in the eyes, a *plink* of a violin string is heard. And if he punches Curly in the stomach, you know you're going to hear the *thud* of a bass drum. Parents in the 1960s (including my own) were up in arms about their kids being exposed to such "violence." If only they could have foreseen the *genuine* violence that would one day threaten the lives of the nation's school-aged children, they wouldn't have given a moment's thought to a harmless kiddie show. But, to that earlier generation of parents and teachers, the Stooges were Public Enemies number One, Two, and Three. On

May 7, 1970, a day that has lived in infamy, independently owned stations across the country banned The Three Stooges' shorts from the airwaves.

Without their reassuring presence at the end of a school day, I often wondered what had become of the Stooges—not their films, but the men themselves. This is what I learned in 1973.

Moe Howard, seventy-six, lived with his wife of nearly fifty years, the former Helen Schonberger, in a modern home overlooking West Hollywood's Sunset Strip. Unlike his surviving partners, Moe was wealthy, having invested in California real estate. A man of intense energy, he continued to look for every opportunity to perform—and get paid to do it. One lucrative outlet for him was giving lectures at colleges. The students hung on his every word and loudly applauded his recreating various Stooge routines, playing all three roles himself. He was also an occasional guest on *The Mike Douglas Show*, although he once told me during a phone call that he declined the offer to be one of Mike's co-hosts, which would have entailed his appearing on the ninety-minute show every day for a week. "I don't want to wear out my welcome," he said with genuine humility. Moe gave numerous interviews, during which he would sometimes reminisce about his childhood. One anecdote concerned his mother's preference for keeping her young son's hair long, almost to shoulder length. Moe said that because of this fashion statement, every weekday he was forced to fight his way "*to* school, *in* school, and *back home from* school." Fed up with being chided by his male classmates, he took a pair of shears and cut his hair straight across and around the back, creating the Moe Howard haircut. Even in his seventies, he retained his signature look, although he stopped dying his hair. He had also retained his expertise at pie-throwing. To prove it, a table had been set up with several pies, allowing him to demonstrate his various techniques on a mannequin. When this was met with only polite laughter, he dis-

Moe Howard. Photo courtesy of Scott H. Reboul.

pensed with the dummy and took aim at Mike's other guests. By the show's end, everyone on the stage was plastered with gooey whipped cream and the studio audience was in hysterics.

Joe Besser, sixty-six, just so happened to know my aunt Agnes. She worked as a checker in a North Hollywood grocery store, and he regularly came through her line. While ringing up his order, she told him about her old-movie-obsessed nephew. Joe wrote down his address and phone number and told Agnes that he wanted to hear from me. I was only too happy to

Joe Besser. Photo courtesy of Scott H. Reboul.

oblige. Joe had a long and varied career in show business. He appeared in vaudeville, on Broadway, radio, television, and in motion picture shorts and features. I especially enjoyed his hilariously toxic character Stinky Davis on *The Abbott and Costello Show*. And, at least for a brief time, he was a Stooge, although he never really felt comfortable with their roughneck style of comedy. Currently, he was a voice actor for a Saturday morning cartoon show. Per Joe's request, I sent him a typical fan letter and immediately received a gracious, typed reply. Also enclosed in the envelope was an autographed publicity photo that included his trademark line, "Not so LOUD!" I followed this up with a phone call, which was a far more immediate experience. His wife since 1932, Ernie, the former Erna Kay Kretschmer, answered. I asked if I could speak with Joe. "Certainly," she said. I could hear her calling, "JOEY!" followed by his unmistakably high-pitched voice responding, "WHATEE?" He was a nice man, a tad prickly, but when he was in a good mood he didn't mind doing some of his catch phrases, including the aforementioned "Not so LOUD!" and "Oh, you crazy!"

Curly-Joe DeRita, sixty-four, lived just a few blocks away from Joe Besser in a modest home he had purchased from Moe. Hired originally for his superficial resemblance to the corpulent Curly Howard, he had become obese in retirement. He also had extremely poor vision, which kept him close to home and

Curly-Joe DeRita. Photo courtesy of Scott H. Reboul.

under the watchful care of his second wife, Jean. (His first wife, Bonnie, had died in 1965; he married Jean in 1966.) A man with an offbeat sense of humor, he liked to shock unsuspecting visitors by answering the front door wearing little more than his underpants. ("What's the big deal?" he would say. "They're clean.") In 1978, one of the mail-order film merchants I dealt with was Mike Lefebvre, who apparently knew the DeRitas. Mike and a group of fellow Stooge fans were planning to pay the aging comedian a visit and he invited me to join them. The thought of seeing Curly-Joe "in the flesh," as it were, was all I needed to decline Mike's offer.

Larry Fine, a seventy-one-year-old widower, had suffered a career-ending stroke in January 1970. Once he was released from the hospital, he went to live at his daughter Phyllis's home, in an apartment above her garage. He soon realized that he needed more

Larry Fine. Photo courtesy of Scott H. Reboul.

care, including intensive physical rehabilitation. This he found in full measure at the Motion Picture Home's newly constructed lodge. Partially paralyzed and confined to a wheelchair, Larry refused to let these inconveniences slow him down. He was usually up for a game of shuffleboard, a craft project, or watching the latest movie at the campus theatre. The best-known and most popular resident at the Home, he entertained his dining room companions with jokes, and always wore the most outrageous costume in the annual wheelchair parade; one year he went as the titular character from the 1962 shocker *What Ever Happened to Baby Jane?* He also welcomed some famous visitors, including the Stooges' former producer/director Jules White, "Mister Television" Milton Berle, and "Yankee Doodle Dandy" actor James Cagney. Moe showed up as well, and even performed skits with Larry in the residents' variety shows.

Following my annual visit with Uncle Ted, this time on Saturday, November 24, 1973, I walked in almost pitch darkness across the dimly lit campus from the hospital to the lodge. Once there, I asked the nurse on duty if I could meet Larry Fine. She promptly went to his door and knocked on it.

"Come in," I heard him call out.

When she opened the door, I could see that Larry was seated in a brown leather chair, watching television.

"Hello, Larry," I said. "Would it be okay if I came in and talked with you for a few minutes?"

"You might as well," he said, turning off the evening news with a remote control, "there's nothing good on anyway."

Larry was shorter than I expected: like Moe, he was only five-feet-four-inches tall. An even bigger surprise involved his hair. Once an unmanageable bush of auburn curls, it was now shorn, greying, and combed back in a dignified manner. His rapid-fire delivery had slowed and was somewhat garbled due to the stroke. He was also nine years older than the reference books alleged. Despite the ravages of time and ill health, it was still

Larry, still the same man whose face belonged with the other Stooges on the comedy version of Mount Rushmore.

I took a mental note of my surroundings. The room had a double bed upon which rested a few stuffed animals. Staring down from the walls were some black-and-white glossies and fan drawings of Larry and his partners in their prime. His long writing desk was littered with mail from admirers around the globe. Also on his desk was a framed photograph dating back to his earliest days in vaudeville. Larry was recognizable as a diminutive teenager holding a violin in a group shot. He noticed that I was looking at the faded picture.

"Would you believe that that is me—?"

"When you were part of the Gus Edwards Newsboy Sextet in 1915," I said with some authority.

Larry seemed taken aback. "Yeah," he said.

I explained that I had made a study of American vaudeville. This reminded Larry of George Jessel, who started with Gus Edwards around the same time as he. Larry then showed me a copy of that day's local newspaper, which had a photo taken at the annual Thanksgiving Day meal at the Friars Club. It was of Larry being pushed in his wheelchair by the seventy-five-year-old Jessel. Something about that photo bothered me. It turned out to be the look of pitying condescension on Jessel's face. Because I was born without a censor button, I said softly, "I don't like him." Larry looked up at me and said in a near whisper, "Neither do I."

That kind of honesty made Larry a compelling conversationalist. When I ventured that I had seen Moe on *The Mike Douglas Show* and that he seemed youthful still, he said, "People are always saying that Moe looks young; I think he looks *old!*" He was critical of his own appearance as well. "Have you seen pictures of me from just before I got sick?" he asked me. "I could have passed for fifty!" He said that due to his sedentary lifestyle and high-calorie diet he had become overweight. (Larry told me that his favorite dish in the Home's dining room was Tomato Surprise—the surprise is that it was stuffed with tuna salad.)

More than anything, he was critical of his own voice, which had been affected by the stroke. As he said, "I don't belong in show business with my voice in this condition."

Suddenly, there came a loud buzzing from the nightstand intercom.

He reached over and flipped a switch. "Yeah?" he said.

"Mister Fine," a female voice intoned, "you have a caller on line three."

"Okay."

One amenity not offered by the Home was a private telephone in each room. Residents were expected to speak on various communal phones located in the halls outside the living quarters.

I assisted Larry into his wheelchair and took him to the nearest phone. When he was poised to lift the receiver, I offered my goodbyes.

Larry touched me on the arm. "You don't really have to go, do you?"

"I guess not," I answered.

"Let me just take this call," he said, "and then we can really *talk*."

And we did: sometimes in his room, occasionally through letters, but mostly during my weekly Saturday afternoon calls with him. Despite our fifty-seven-year age difference, Larry and I discovered that we had more in common than just a mutual interest in comedy. We were both born in the eastern part of the United States and now lived in the West; we were both animal lovers; we both liked to draw; and neither one of us had a particularly strong attention span when it came to serious matters.

In August 1974, I spent an entire week as a guest at Aunt Agnes's house in the San Fernando Valley. Without anybody telling me when to turn in for the night, I watched movie marathons on KTTV Channel 11, from midnight to six in the morning. The only drawback to that were the frequent, annoying-as-hell commercials by used car salesman Cal Worthington ("Go see Cal, go see

Cal, go see Cal!"). I was usually awakened at the crack of noon by the incessant barking of Scruffy, the Wirehaired Terrier next door. Like seemingly everyone else in L.A., Scruffy was an out-of-work actor, having been the family dog on *The Ghost and Mrs. Muir*. While eating a healthy breakfast (usually a Pop Tart and a 7up), I would watch back-to-back butchered Stooge shorts on KBSC-TV, Channel 52. My newly married cousin Susan, whose former bedroom I was inhabiting, would stop by after work and drive me to Woodland Hills, where I could visit at leisure with my friends at the Home.

Larry often told interviewers that he disliked watching himself, but I can tell you this was not the case. He loved seeing the Stooges and he chuckled at every little joke and bit of business. In those days, long before VCRs, I made audio recordings of various scenes in sound comedies being shown on television. In this case, I had recorded the Stooges' cameo appearance in the 1963 comedy-western *4 for Texas*, starring Frank Sinatra, Dean Martin, Anita Eckberg, and Ursula Andress. Set in Galveston in 1870, Martin plays the owner of a newly refurbished riverboat casino. On opening day, three inept moving men (guess who) have been promised two dollars to deliver a large nude painting of the owner's curvaceous girlfriend (Ursula Andress). Protestors in the form of two pious old ladies (Jesslyn Fax and Ellen Corby) show up, one pushing the other in a wheelchair, to vehemently object to the painting's public display. A confrontation takes place between the reformers in widow's weeds, and Moe, Larry, and Curly-Joe. Larry is at first solicitous of the wheelchair-ridden woman, saying she reminds him of his mother. When she relentlessly beats Moe over the head with an umbrella, Larry adds with perfect timing: "I *told* you she reminds me of my mother!" Curly-Joe unwittingly retaliates by pushing the woman out of her chair. In their well-crafted three minutes of screen time, the Stooges perform two of their stock routines, "Point to the right" and "Insulting the state of (*clap, clap, clap*) Texas."

Larry listened attentively, a crooked smile brightening his face. He said that Dean Martin, who at one point gives the Boys a "triple slap," told them it was the funniest thing he had ever seen them do. Given Larry's current status as a "differently abled" American, I asked him what he thought of the lady being pushed out of the wheelchair. Thinking it was Ellen Corby who landed on the ground, he said, "Hell, she's doin' better than *I* am." (At that time, Ellen Corby was a series regular on *The Waltons*.) He then recalled a similar sequence in another 1963 release, *The Three Stooges Go Around the World in a Daze*, when a heavyset woman (Audrey Betz) repeatedly bangs him on the head with her purse. "She kept hitting me and hitting me with that purse and it felt like she had a gun in it. I finally said, '*Jesus Christ, lady, cut it out!*'"

Another sound clip I played for him was from a recent episode of *All in the Family*, a show he and I both loved. Edith and Archie Bunker (Jean Stapleton and Carroll O'Connor) are in a hotel room on their second honeymoon. Hoping for a romantic evening, Edith overhears her husband refer to an entry in the *TV Guide*: "Hey, will ya' look at dis—the Tree Stooges is on tonight!" Larry got a huge kick out of that.

I made those recordings for him because he was unhappy that the Home did not offer cable television to the residents, thereby depriving him of seeing his old films on a daily basis. He told me he was tempted to hire someone on the sly to hook it up for him, but that never happened. His only other option was to watch one of his own 16mm prints he kept in his room, provided somebody else operated the projector. Being a film collector from way back, I told him I could work it. Then, after taking a closer look at the machine, I saw just how different it was from my old TSI model. For some unknown reason, Larry was under the impression that I was mechanically inclined. One day he told me to improve the reception on his television while he was out of his room; there was a Los Angeles Dodgers game coming on soon and he wanted the picture to come in as clear as possible. This was when televisions had antennae, or rabbit ears, as they were commonly called. I adjusted the wires this way and that, and the picture looked steadily worse. When he wheeled himself in about twenty minutes later, he took one look at the picture and said, "Is that the best you could do?"

Now I had committed myself to operating his projector, and I didn't want to disappoint him. First, I had to produce a blank spot on the white wall to serve as a screen. Larry had a large, framed certificate of appreciation that had been presented to him by some junior high school. Knowing he was especially proud of it, I approached it with care. What I didn't know was that it was attached to the wall by masking tape. When the tape came off, a wide piece of dried paint came with it.

"Sorry," I said.

He just looked at me.

Now for the projector. I held up the 800-foot reel and unraveled some of the film's leader. I should have realized that a cut was needed on the first frame for it to fit the projector's aperture. Instead, I fed the uncircumcised film into the machine and waited for it to come out near the take-up reel. Worried that it was taking too long to come out the other side, I opened the side panel, which covered the mechanism. The film, not surprisingly, was jammed in the gate. The only thing I could do was to manually extract it, which I knew could damage the print. I turned to Larry for reassurance.

He just looked at me.

I was getting exasperated with my own ineptitude. Meeting his gaze, I said, "Larry, I can't do this."

For the first and only time, he became stern with me.

"Never say *can't*." he admonished. "When I had my stroke, I had to relearn how to do everything, including dressing myself. I was so frustrated that I called my daughter and said, 'Come and get me; I can't do it.' Just then, a physical therapist—a great big guy—walked in and stood over me. 'You can do it,' he said. 'And I'm not leaving here until you're done.' It took a long time, and I looked at him pleadingly, but all he would say was 'Keep going; you're doing great.' I kept going, and I *finally* succeeded. If *I* can do it, so can *you*."

Larry might have been past doing slapstick comedy, but he could have had a second career as a motivational speaker.

I was suddenly suffused with renewed determination. "Let me *at* this thing," I said. Just then, I noticed a small booklet attached to the projector's case. The instructions. *Why* hadn't I thought to read those first? I picked up the booklet to read about properly loading the film in the self-threading aperture. My hands were shaking a bit, and I dropped the booklet. It landed at Larry's feet. Being a gentleman, he bent over to pick it up. I had the same idea. Our heads banged together, and I do mean *hard*. It occurred to me that I had just bumped heads with one of The Three Stooges,

The author is jubilant to be in the company of one of his comic heroes, Larry Fine of The Three Stooges.

and I laughed myself sick. Far less amused, Larry was cursing a blue streak. As embarrassed as I was for failing so miserably as a projectionist, I said to him, "After all the dumb things I've seen you do in films, I can't feel *too* bad about myself."

"That may be," he said as he rubbed his sore noggin, "but at least *I got paid* to make an ass of *my*self."

One of Larry's friends at the Home was Babe London. I was familiar with her from her supporting roles with Laurel & Hardy and the Stooges; she had also been a comedienne in the silent era. When Larry was invited to appear at area schools, he would sometimes invite Babe along, and she always went—she *loved* being recognized. She had a way of knowing when Larry had a visitor; it's possible she had a spy working for her at the lodge. One lazy afternoon, while Larry was dozing in his chair and I was lying on his bed, reading, a nurse entered the room to relay a message: Babe London wanted Larry's young guest to pay her a visit. Without waking my host, I asked the nurse for directions to Babe's cottage.

She greeted me warmly, displaying a wide smile that made her eyes look like two slits. At seventy-three, she was tall, a bit less plump than I remembered her, and she had obviously just fixed her hair and freshened her lipstick.

"Miss London, it's a pleasure to meet you," I said sincerely.

"Oh, *please*, it's Babe. That's what *all* my friends call me."

Babe ushered me into her small living room, where she offered me a refreshing glass of iced tea. We talked about her life and career, and what she told me was quite interesting.

She was born Jean Glover in Des Moines, Iowa, on September 28, 1901. When she was in her teens, her family, including one brother, moved to San Diego. A student at San Diego High School, she heard her female classmates talking about the movies they had seen. Each of these sylphs believed with all her heart that she could be the next Lillian Gish. But being in the movies held no special allure for the full-figured Jean. More than anything, she wanted to study art and become a painter. One afternoon, she happened upon a small moving picture company at work in a park. A member of the crew noticed her and said, rather indelicately, that they needed a fat girl for the next scene—would she mind? Before she knew what was happening, she found herself engaged for the part. Even if *she* didn't want the movies, the movies evidently wanted *her*. And considering how easy she found her first experience to be, she began to think acting might not be such a bad way to earn her tuition at a good art school. She went to Los Angeles, where she found plenty of opportunities for a fat, funny girl in pictures. Using the nickname "Babe" (not unlike Oliver "Babe" Hardy), and the last name London (not unlike the foggy town in England), she got her first major breaks in 1919 by working for two of the biggest stars in Hollywood: Douglas Fairbanks and Charlie Chaplin. She played a telephone operator in Doug's Triangle feature comedy *When the Clouds Roll By*, and a seasick ferry passenger in Charlie's First National two-reeler *A Day's Pleasure*. I asked her what it was like to be directed by the Great Chaplin.

"Oh, he was very nice," she said, smiling at the memory. "We did one scene together, with close-ups and everything. When we finished filming, he put his hand on my shoulder and said, 'Babe, if you stick by this, you're going to make it.' That was so encouraging!"

That prophecy proved correct. Before long, she was one of the busiest comediennes in pictures. Her catchy name and smiling face were also popping up in ads and articles in trade magazines. One article, entitled "Worth Their Weight in Gold," highlighted some of the screen's plus-sized comics, including Joe Cobb of Our Gang, Nellie Lane, and Walter Hiers, who were then tickling the masses' collective funny bone. Babe and Walter were said to be "adding weight to the Christie Comedies." Al and Charles Christie, two brothers from Canada, understood the comic possibilities of extreme opposites. The concept no doubt inspired their decision to pair hefty Babe with the slender Dorothy DeVore. One surviving example of their two-reelers is *Kidding Katie* (1923). The

Babe London submits to a bike-riding lesson from her co-star Al St. John in the extant two-reeler Red Pepper *(1925). Courtesy of Randy Skretvedt.*

scenario concerns two privileged sisters, Queenie (Babe) and Katie (Dorothy).

Queenie has been corresponding for years with a man she considers her beau (James Harrison), although he has never laid eyes on her. When the mischievous Katie slips a picture of her fine self in one of Queenie's letters, the man shows up at their front door to claim his bride. The girls' mother insists that Katie dress as a little girl in rompers to serve as a deterrent, but the letter-writing Lothario readily sees through this farcical disguise. He and Katie become a couple, much to Queenie's chagrin.

Interestingly, Babe and Dorothy aren't the only disparate-looking duo in the film. Diminutive Billy Bletcher is the family's butler, and Blanche Payson, the six-foot-two former policewoman, is a housemaid. This eye-catching pair competes with the leads for laughs.

Although a success in shorts, Babe fared less well in features. Her single scene in the Harry Langdon *noir* comedy *Long Pants* (1927) was still on the cutting-room floor when the film was being shown in theatres. The same fate befell her scene in the Buster Keaton seven-reeler *Go West* (1925). One part she played that she might have *wished* had been cut was that of a circus strong woman in *Tillie's Punctured Romance* (1928). Not to be confused with the seminal 1914 Keystone comedy feature starring Marie Dressler, Mabel Normand, and Charlie Chaplin, this *Tillie's Punctured Romance* starred the short-lived team of W.C. Fields and Chester Conklin, with Louise Fazenda as the eponymous Tillie. Actress Louise Brooks, whose husband Eddie Sutherland was the picture's director, wrote that it "was filmed with groans, previewed with moans, and then buried in the vaults. Tillie had not a single mourner."

In addition to her film work, Babe appeared in vaudeville, where she displayed her talent for singing. It was there that she had her first exposure to Stan Laurel. He was performing in a sketch called "The Burglar," and it made a favorable impression on her. She would work with Stan in 1923 in *The Handy Man*, one of the many solo two-reelers he made prior to teaming with Oliver Hardy. When the team starred in their 1931 talkie *Our Wife*, Stan knew that Babe London would be ideal as Ollie's zaftig fian-

The climactic wedding sequence from Our Wife. *Left to right: Stan Laurel, Oliver Hardy, Ben Turpin, Babe London, and Blanche Payson.*

Babe London visits with Stan Laurel at the Oceana Hotel, located at 849 Ocean Avenue, apt. 203, in Santa Monica, in 1961. Courtesy of Letters from Stan: The Stan Laurel Correspondence Archive Project.

cée, Dulcie, the pampered daughter of excitable tycoon James Finlayson.

Stan and Ollie are preparing for a wedding reception in their home when Dulcie telephones. Clearly distraught, she tells Ollie that her father does not approve of him as a potential son-in-law. She tearfully adds that he has locked her in her room. "*Ohhhh*," she wails, "what are we going to do?" Ollie assuredly states that there is only one thing *to* do: they will elope! Instantly pacified, Dulcie responds, "How *romantic*!" In the next scene, Ollie is placing a ladder against the Finlayson mansion, on which Dulcie descends from her bedroom window. Best Man Stanley, who had been put in charge of renting a limousine for this special occasion, shows up with a tiny automobile known as an Austin. Getting into the car is a struggle, but they finally succeed. Their next stop, late into the night, is the home of Justice of the Peace William Gladding. The judge's disagreeable wife (Blanche Payson again) summons her husband from the bedroom. (Gladding is none other than Ben Turpin, the cross-eyed comic of many a Mack Sennett production.) He unintelligibly performs the ceremony and then, due to his ocular condition, weds Ollie to Stanley. Out of camera range, Dulcie screams and faints.

The sequence in which Stan helps the king-sized prospective bride and groom into the vehicle is one of the funniest sustained routines in the Laurel & Hardy canon. I specifically asked Babe about shooting that particular sequence. She and I laughed just thinking about it.

"Somebody else was credited as the director [James W. Horne]," she said, "but Stan was really the one who directed that whole scene. And as you know, Stan didn't like to over-rehearse; he said it cut down on spontaneity. Then, he would ad-lib while the camera was rolling. You know the part where he pushes Hardy and me into the car? I had *no* idea he was going to do that!

We had to push our faces up against the car windows to make it seem even smaller than it was—and it was already pretty small! I don't think we did more than one or two takes on any scene. With Stan in charge, everything went very smoothly."

Regarding the other venerable comedic actors in the film, Babe had nothing but fond memories: "Ben Turpin didn't need to work—he was pretty well off, I guess—but Stan decided that no one else could play the part of the cross-eyed judge. Ben was very nice. Jimmy Finlayson and Blanche Payson were, too."

Babe so enjoyed Stan's company that she kept in touch with him for the rest of his life, paying visits to the apartment he shared with his wife, Ida, in Santa Monica. The two-time co-stars even made a home movie in which they pretend to sit down to watch a Laurel & Hardy short on television, using a doctored *TV Guide* as a prop. Babe was bowled over by Stan's sharp wit, which, she always pointed out to interviewers, was antithetical to his vacuous screen image.

Like *Our Wife*, The Three Stooges short *Scrambled Brains* (1951) revolves around a wedding.

> It begins with Shemp being discharged from a sanitarium, where he underwent treatment for hallucinations. Apparently, the treatment was inadequate, considering the surreal visions still being conjured up by his addled mind. At one point, he is playing the piano; when he looks down, he sees two sets of hands on the keyboard. The most potent hallucination involves his nurse, Nora (Babe). He perceives her as a cool beautiful blonde, not the bombastic, hideous-looking woman she really is. She seems to be missing all her teeth, with the exception of two fanglike incisors. Moe and Larry try to help their friend see reason, but he is hopelessly smitten. Out of options, they agree to hold a reception for the soon-to-be newlyweds. During their return trip from the grocery store, they have a messy encounter in a phone booth with a hostile fat man (Vernon Dent). The results are so cataclysmic that the man threatens to tear Larry and

Moe limb from limb if he ever sees them again. Back at the apartment, now occupied by Moe, Larry, Shemp, and the grotesquely dolled-up Nora, the father of the bride arrives. Predictably enough, it is the same angry individual with whom the Boys had just tussled. Chaos ensues. Punches are thrown. Nora, with her unconscious fiancé slung over her shoulder, departs while wordlessly singing "Here Comes the Bride."

Babe was very open when discussing her weight: she cheerfully admitted to having been 255 pounds at her peak. This assured her of being called when comedy producers needed that type. But when she was diagnosed with a heart condition, her physician urged her to lose at least 100 pounds. Her health may have improved but she had lost the gimmick that made her castable. She was also getting older and finding the same difficulty experienced by most actresses over thirty in the movie capital. Aside from the aforementioned classic short comedies, Babe's career in sound films did not produce any other memorable titles. Well, maybe one: *Sex Kittens Go to College* (1960), an ultra-low budget exploitation flick, written and directed by Albert Zugsmith for Allied Artists. Set in a college populated by busty blondes, including Mamie Van Doren, it also features a ragtag group of guest stars: old-timers John Carradine and Jackie Coogan, and neophytes with legendary names, Charlie Chaplin Jr. and Harold Lloyd Jr. For her contribution, Babe essays the role of Miss Cadwallader, a prim spinster. This cinematic hodgepodge is ninety-four minutes long, although there was a second version for foreign markets. Lasting 103 minutes, it featured unrelated clips of striptease artists plying their trade.

Babe tried other pursuits, all without much success. She mentioned that she had wanted to establish a weight loss clinic and spa in Hawaii, but without investors she could not move forward. Without going into the gory details, she said she had been married twice, with both unions ending in divorce. For a time, she wrote a column geared toward senior citizens, or *Senior Americans*, her preferred term. When asked what she planned to write about, she answered: "I'll explore their hobbies, accomplishments, problems, their philosophy, and entire way of life in what I like to call their 'Golden Harvest Years.'"

In her early sixties, Babe began preparing for her own years as a Senior American by applying for admittance to the Motion Picture Home. Ironically, her cottage was adjacent to her former Christie partner Dorothy DeVore. Some unpleasantness marred their working relationship and the memory of it did not fade over time. As a result, the two women never exchanged a word.

Like many of her contemporaries, Babe did not believe the slogan "Movies Are Better Than Ever." As she wistfully told me, "It was so warm and welcoming in the silent days. But in the recent films I've been in, the atmosphere is more like a factory, with lots of pressure and everyone worrying about time and money." She paused and took a sip of iced tea. "Now, the only time we old movie people get together is at funerals. I went to Mack Sennett's ... Babe Hardy's ... Stan's ... Buster's ..." Her voice trailed off. "It really is a vanishing era, isn't it?"

Babe found immense satisfaction pursuing her original goal by taking an adult education art class, where she learned the basics of painting. As a tribute to her comrades in comedy, she undertook a series of portraits—everyone from Laurel & Hardy to Chaplin to lesser-known funny men and women. Appropriately enough, she called the series, "The Vanishing Era." They were clearly painted with love, and she was proud of them. One is of Chester Conklin, the prominent Keystone player with the sad eyes and a whiskbroom mustache. Chester had passed away, at the age of eighty-five, at the Motion Picture Hospital on October 11, 1971. Babe shared a personal memory with me about the memorial service held in his honor. "At one point," she said with a grin, "somebody loudly popped open a bottle of champagne. I could almost hear Chester's laugh when that happened."

It had been a lovely visit—a bit melancholy, but lovely. Babe graciously inscribed a copy of *Pratfall*, the official newsletter of

Babe London poses with some of the paintings from her series, "The Vanishing Era." Courtesy of the Media History Digital Library.

the Laurel & Hardy appreciation group, The Sons of the Desert, named after their 1933 feature. On the cover, she wrote: "To one of my nicest fans. Sincerely, Babe London."

Several months after our visit, Babe married for the third, and final, time. The groom was fellow resident Phil Boutelje, a retired musician, songwriter, composer, author, and conductor. She was clearly smitten with this accomplished gentleman. I ran into the happy couple one day when they were out taking a constitutional. Babe proudly introduced him to me.

"You're marrying a winner," I said as I shook his hand.

"*He's* the winner," Babe said as little cartoon hearts encircled her dreamy expression.

They had been husband and wife for four years when Phil died on July 29, 1979, just days prior to his eighty-fourth birthday. As for Babe, she was less afraid of dying than she was of being forgotten. The antidote for this came in the form of a personal visit from historian and archivist Gene M. Gressley. Gene was approaching various individuals at the Home about the possibility of their bequeathing their show business memorabilia to the American Heritage Center at the University of Wyoming. Most likely, Babe simply said, "Where do I sign?" Knowing that her legacy would be assured, she passed away peacefully on November 29, 1980, at the age of seventy-nine. The boxes containing her personal effects—fifteen in all, measuring 9.3 cubic feet, and a separate shipment of seventy-five paintings—soon began arriving at the university in Laramie. There were photo albums, scrapbooks, original movie posters and stills, 8- and 16mm prints of her films, audio tapes, and correspondence. There was an additional item not to be found in the inventory for collection 05192. It was an urn containing Babe's cremains. Apparently, she wanted to spend eternity among her souvenirs.

Coda

Nineteen seventy-four was, in many ways, the apex of my rubbing shoulders (and bumping heads) with celebrities of the past. But just as the Lord giveth, the Lord taketh away. Bud Abbott, Lou Costello's brilliant straight man, who was someone I had written to and very much wanted to meet, died on April 24, 1974, at the age of seventy-six. My uncle Ted Edlin, that poor man, died at seventy-nine on July 7. Robert Cox, one of the last original Keystone Kops and a good friend of mine, died suddenly on September 8; he too was seventy-nine. And on December 26, the same sad day that Jack Benny left us, seventy-two-year-old Larry Fine suffered a second major stroke and lapsed into a coma.

I had heard that comatose patients are often fully aware and benefit greatly from verbal stimulation. I therefore made a pledge to myself that I would write a letter of encouragement to Larry every day until he was well again. Recovery would be an uphill battle, I realized, but I also knew how determined he could be. For the next three weeks, I pestered the staff in the hospital's J Ward for updates. On some days, the doctors were hopeful, detecting signs of movement from the patient; on other days, he was unresponsive. Eventually, he was taken off his feeding tube and he died, just before dawn, on January 24, 1975. Nurse Marianne told me that she had finished reading the last of my letters to him only moments before he passed away.

I skipped school to attend his funeral in the Church of the Recessional at Forest Lawn in Glendale. It was held at ten o'clock on January 27, which happened to be a drizzly Monday morning. Because I could neither drive nor find someone to take me to L.A., I arrived by Greyhound bus. I was dropped off at the massive front gates of the cemetery with only minutes to spare. For the first (and only) time in my life I actually hitchhiked. A carful of Good Samaritans kindly gave me the needed lift. The rabbi's eulogy was lighthearted, as Larry would have wanted. Seeing my friend with his eyes closed reminded me of the times he dozed off in my presence; it made me feel good that he was comfortable enough around me to do so. The entombment took place in Forest Lawn's modern Freedom Mausoleum, in the Sanctuary of Liberation, Crypt 22217. There were some familiar faces in the small gathering, including Jules White and one of the Three Stooges' most prolific foils, Emil Sitka. Sadly, seventy-seven-year-old Moe Howard, who had been diagnosed with lung cancer, was unable to attend the service. He followed his partner in death just four months later, on May 4, 1975.

They're gone, all of those marvelous men and women who entertained generations of moviegoers. But they live on in their films.

The author pays his respects to his late friend Larry Fine in the Freedom Mausoleum at Forest Lawn-Glendale, August 2019. Photo by Christopher Blabac, R.N.

THREE

Mary MacLaren: A Petal on the Current

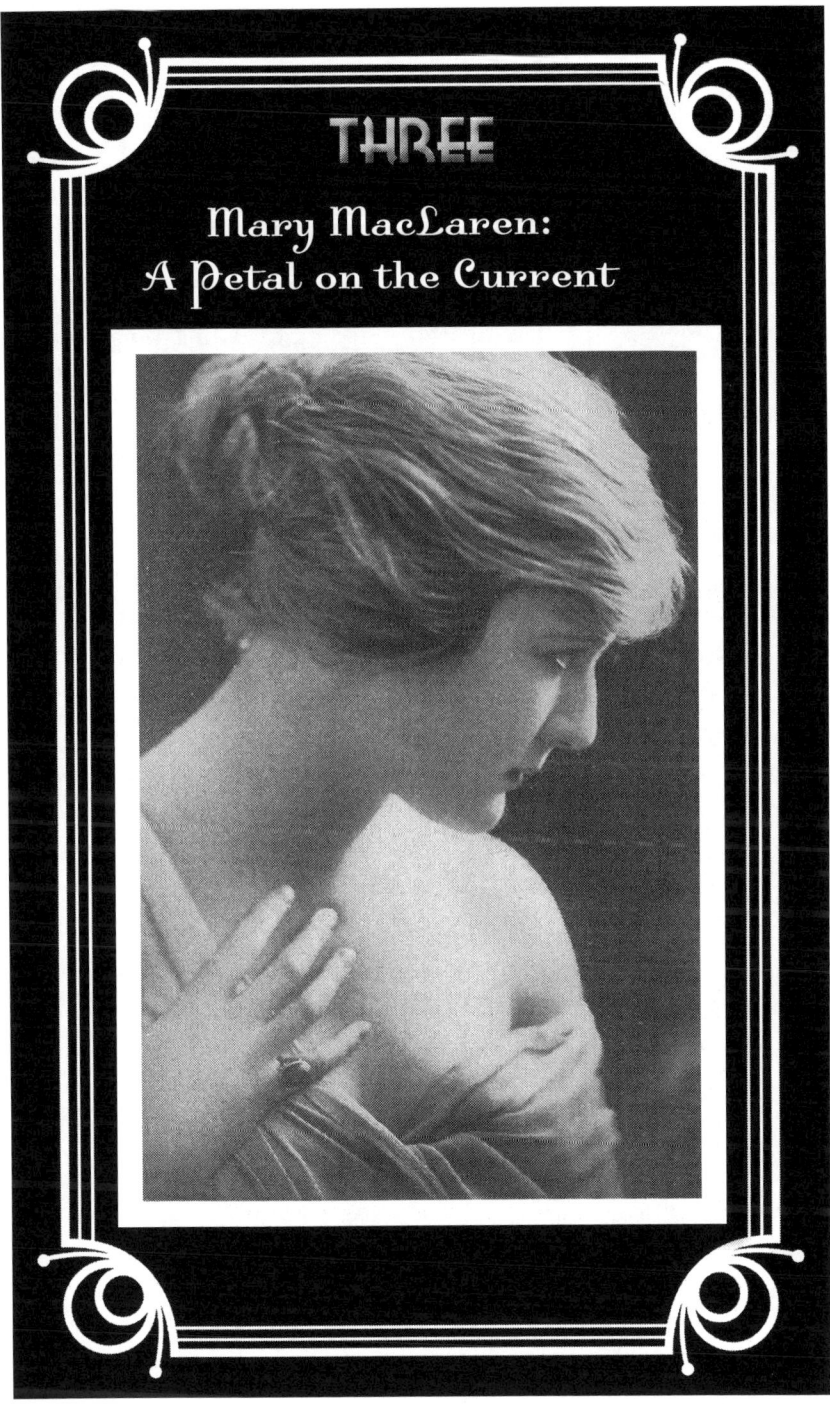

Courtesy of the Media History Digital Library.

Back in the seventies, getting mail (physical mail, not email) was among my greatest joys, particularly if it was a film print I had ordered.

On a spring day in 1975, I saw the mail truck on our street and crossed my fingers, hoping there might be something waiting for me in the box—and there was. It was a package, postmarked Washington, D.C., and it had several of the newly issued D.W. Griffith commemorative stamps in its upper right-hand corner. In the package was an engraved plaque; there was also a cover letter from the sender, Thomas Fulbright. Tom was a bit of an odd duck, I must say, a strange combination of a fey old Southerner and a hawkish opportunist. If he is remembered even slightly by the silent film community, it would be as the creator of the Rosemary Award. This well-intentioned honor was periodically bestowed on the mostly forgotten, and rapidly diminishing, roster of living silent film actresses. The award's name was derived from a passage in *Hamlet*, Act IV, Scene V: "There's Rosemary—That's for Remembrance!" Tom had learned of my existence from his longtime friend Beverly Bayne, and based on their conversations, he assumed I was well connected. In his letter, which must have been typed on the first typewriter ever made (with the original ribbon), he informed me that I had been chosen as the designated presenter of the Rosemary to a once-heralded motion picture actress. Her name was Mary MacLaren.

Perhaps I should have been flattered that he wanted *me*, a sixteen-year-old high school student, to do the honors. My biggest qualm was that he also expected me to turn it into a media event, with plenty of television and newspaper coverage. In many ways a typical kid, I didn't have the wherewithal to arrange this at the level he was expecting. When I asked him how to go about such a task, he replied, "I'm leaving ALL that to you." Another qualm stemmed from the still-fresh memory of the Beverly Bayne tribute screening debacle, something I had no desire to repeat. I also knew next to nothing about Mary MacLaren, although I had only recently seen her as Queen Anne of Austria in Douglas Fairbanks's production of *The Three Musketeers* (1921). I tried to get out of the commitment by saying I had too much school homework, and offered to return the package to him, but Tom turned a deaf ear to me. Never having been on the West Coast in all his sixty-plus years, he considered Los Angeles, where the honoree lived, to be practically next door to me. In fact, it was a two-hour drive from my family's home in San Diego County, and I didn't yet have a learner's permit. But the award was already in my hands, and I was stuck. Usually conscientious to a fault, I did what virtually any adolescent male would do in similar circumstances: nothing. Well, not exactly *nothing*; I *did* read up on Mary's life and career, and it is, I think you'll agree, quite the soap opera.

William Albert MacDonald worked in the coal industry of Pittsburgh, Pennsylvania, before switching to the more genteel field of hotel management. His wife, the former Lillian Agnew, gave up her career as a dancer and actress to assist him in running the hotel. The enterprise was not a success; there were unpaid bills and mounting debt. Closing the hotel, William kept the bar open until his excessive drinking doomed that venture as well. Lillian, realizing she had married an alcoholic ne'er-do-well, filed for divorce in 1902, citing "indignities to the person," whatever that means. Living on the charity of wealthy relatives, Lillian and her three daughters—Catherine (b. 1891), Miriam (b. 1896), and Mary Ida (b. 1900)—used their individual skills to get by. Katherine, who had changed the spelling of her first name from a "C" to a "K," was a natural beauty with theatrical aspirations. She went to New York City to pursue a career as a model, dancer, and singer. Before long, she was cast in *The Passing Show of 1914*, starring Al Jolson, at the Winter Garden Theatre at 50th and Broadway. At the time, Mary was enrolled in a convent in Virginia. When she came home for the Christmas break, it was suggested by her mother that she and her girls pay a visit to Katherine in the big city. The moment Mary set foot in her sister's communal dressing room she knew she had found her true calling. Forget the convent; this girl was going into "the show business." With Katherine's recommendation, Mary became a chorus girl at the tender age of thirteen. Miriam, meanwhile, remained at home with Lillian. Katherine, who had been the most emotionally scarred by the family's straitened circumstances (having to wear her cousins' hand-me-downs was an especially despised memory), left the chorus to marry a well-to-do Pittsburgh man. She used her husband's vast resources to raise French bulldogs and show them competitively. Her dogs regularly took honors at the Westminster Kennel Club.

Although Katherine was now a member of high society, the rest of her family was going hungry, and it was incumbent upon the teenaged Mary to support them. This coincided with the family's relocation to California, a move necessitated by Miriam's precarious health. Their new home, on Hollywood Boulevard, was a cramped apartment. While Mary was out pounding the pavement, Lillian sewed dresses and Miriam did the lion's share of the housework. With a letter of recommendation from the East, Mary managed to snag a small role in a revue. When that closed, she had no idea where to turn next. A girlfriend took her to Universal City to meet the Smalleys, a husband-and-wife directing team. Missus Smalley was the pioneering female director Lois Weber. She began her career as an actress in 1908. From 1911 to 1914, she and her husband, Phillips Smalley, wrote and directed one single-reel film per week for the Rex Film Company. A former evangelist, she considered this new medium the ideal platform for her "missionary films," also known as morality plays and message pictures. Clearly the guiding force in her marriage, Weber was known for the controversial subject matter of her films, including abortion and birth control, capital punishment, miscegenation, and drug addiction. In 1916, she became Universal's highest paid director, male or female, and formed her own

A trade journal ad for The Smalleys, i.e., Phillips Smalley (left) and Lois Weber (right). Courtesy of the Media History Digital Library.

production company the following year. An *auteur* in every sense of the word, she wrote her own stories and continuity, selected her cast and planned to the smallest detail the scenic effects. She even wrote the title cards and edited the final cut. For her efforts, she became the lone female member of the Motion Picture Directors' Association.

Mary was pleased to make the Smalleys' acquaintance, but she felt that the impression she made on them was mild at best. Nevertheless, she did manage to be cast in an uncredited bit part as a maid in two of their pictures, *John Needham's Double* and *Where Are My Children?* (both 1916). The small compensation for "working extra" was hardly commensurate with her responsibility as the family breadwinner. Fortunately, her next encounter with the couple turned out to be more significant—*life-changing* may be a better description. And it happened because of the shoes she was wearing. Mary could ill afford a new pair, even when the ones she was wearing had long since seen their day. In a rather pathetic attempt to lengthen their lifespan, she painted the shoes repeatedly, each time a different color and a shade darker. The world at large seemed a shade darker as well. As she explained,

> I was feeling very blue despite the beauty of the distant mountains and the greenness of the nearby hills and the sunlight over everything. I had walked from home to Universal to save my bus fare that morning. I think my dress was a little shabby and I daresay I looked woebegone enough. Anyway, Mister Smalley was talking to Missus Smalley, and she stopped to look over at me. I heard her exclaim, "Shoes!" [She then] came right over to me and said I was exactly the type [to play the lead in the film-in-preparation]. They asked me about my work and experience, and they gave me the story to take home to read. That night I sat up late. I read and re-read that story, until I felt I *was* that very girl. The next morning I met Missus Smalley, and we talked some more.

Weber clearly had an eye for talent. In an interview with Grace Kingsley, she said that she foresaw great things for Mary MacDonald.

"*Who* is Mary MacDonald?" Kingsley asked.

Weber answered, "The luckiest find I ever made."

This was not mere hyperbole. Weber was quoted in *Moving Picture World* as having said, "When the film was run in the Universal projection room, every man in the room fell in love with her. She's only sixteen and beautiful, but more than that, she is the most sensitive and intelligent girl I have ever directed. Her face is a veritable mirror of emotion. This Mary MacDonald was born to be an actress, as you will see."

The executives at Universal agreed with Weber's assessment and signed Mary to a contract at thirty-five dollars a week. They also changed her surname from MacDonald to the less common MacLaren. Her first major production for Lois Weber would be her best: *Shoes*, based on a short story by authoress and suffragist Stella Wynne Herron. Considered for decades to be a lost film, *Shoes*, like its director and star, has been rescued from oblivion. In 2014, the five-reel feature (forty-nine minutes in length) was named to the Library of Congress National Film Registry. A complete 35mm nitrate print underwent a meticulous digital restoration by the Netherlands' EYE Institute and was made available on both DVD and Blu-ray in 2016, the film's centennial. With your kind permission, I will put into words the story of *Shoes*, liberally using Lois Weber's original title cards.

> Sixteen-year-old Eva Mayer (Mary MacLaren) stands before a store window, coveting a pair of new shoes that are on display. Her own pair are badly worn and in need of replacement. Standing beside her is Lil, a co-worker (Jessie Arnold), who reacts positively when she notices the leering glance of one "Cabaret" Charlie (William V. Mong). Eva, the true recipient of his gaze, pays the man no mind and makes her way home. Walking up the stairs to the dark and food-scented hall of the Mayer family's depressing flat, she passes the open door to the room where her father (Harry Griffith) can always be found, in bed, reading the newspaper and fortifying himself with cheap liquor. As she looks at him in disgust, she longs for the strength to seize him, to stand him upright and make him work for his family—under the lash if necessary. In

the kitchen is her hard-working, constantly complaining mother (Mattie Witting) and Eva's three younger sisters (they are unbilled, but one of them is the future silent star Lina Basquette). The air is pungent with the Saturday-night smell of corned beef and cabbage—mostly cabbage. Eva dutifully hands the five one-dollar bills to her mother; it is her weekly salary from the five-and-ten-cent store, where she works as a salesclerk.

Without a word of thanks, her mother pockets the money in her housedress, saying, "That'll just make up the rent. The butcher will have to wait again."

Eva, clearly disappointed, says, "Aren't you going to let me have the three dollars, mama? You know, you promised." To strengthen her appeal, she indicates the poor condition of her footwear.

"You can get them next week—sure," her mother answers somewhat mechanically.

The family gathers at the kitchen table for the consumption of the unappetizing boiled cabbage. The *paterfamilias* takes one last swig before he joins them. It is the master's habit to prop his book against the sugar bowl and read during the meal. The children bicker. Eva, sitting at her place with a sad expression, cannot eat a bite. No one at the table seems to notice, or even care. They've got their own problems.

Monday morning. Eva is carefully cutting out a pair of soles from a cardboard box and inserting them into her shoes. In the kitchen, her mother is beating the same drum about Father's chronic unemployment: "The butcher said Saturday, he won't trust us no more till you got a job." Eva leaves for work, stopping once again to stare longingly at the shoes in the store window.

Lil tells her excitedly, "You know that guy that rubbered us outside the shoe store? Well, I ran into him again yesterday, and he wants to meet you."

But Eva is barely listening. Later that day, Cabaret Charlie is one of the many customers crowding the five-and-dime. Despite Lil's flirty ways, he only has eyes for the comely Eva. "I'm singing down at the Blue Goose," he tells her. "Drop in some time." She continues to give him the cold shoulder.

The following morning is a rainy one. (There is an excellent tracking shot of the backs of Eva's disintegrating shoes in the downpour.) Eva walks to and from work and is truly worse for the wear. She soaks her poor aching feet in a large bowl of steaming water and falls asleep. When her mother awakens her, she ascertains that her daughter is running a fever. Eva's throat is also painful, her glands are swollen, and she has even less of an appetite than usual. That night, she lies awake, worrying about the fate of her family. In an effective superimposition, a large, distorted-looking hand, with the dreaded word POVERTY written on it in ink, lingers over the frightened girl. In the kitchen, her parents argue in hushed tones. There is no need for intertitles. We know what they are saying. The mother, meanwhile, carefully stores every leftover drop of milk.

Eva needs to see a doctor, to get plenty of bedrest and proper nourishment, but what would her family do if she could not bring home that weekly five dollars? Starve, most likely. She stands listlessly behind the counter, feeling her swollen neck glands as Lil expresses her concern. On her lunch break, Eva sits on a park bench, too weak to eat the sandwich her mother had packed for her. People pass by, and they all seem to be well off. Every woman is wearing fashionable new shoes. Almost reflexively, she hides her feet from view. Fortunately, it was that blessed day in which she received her weekly salary. Back at home, she hands her mother the full amount, as always. There is a look of hopeful anticipation on her face, but her mother says nothing.

"Ain't you going to give me the three dollars, mama?"

And the inevitable answer: "I can't do it, child. We've got to eat, and no one will let us have anything more except for cash."

Eva is at her breaking point. She enters her father's bedroom and says without preamble, "I've got to have a new pair of shoes."

He answers by holding up one of his own shoes, pointing to a small hole in it. Then, to appease her, he adds, "I'll be sure to find some work, and I'll give you the money then."

Eva, with her jaw set in grim determination, goes to her room. Taking out a brush, she freshens her hairstyle and changes into her most attractive outfit. Looking down at her unsightly shoes, she loosens her skirt and lowers it until it skims the floor, thus obscuring them completely. Coiffed and behatted, she stares for a few moments into a small mirror, examining her reflection. There is a crack in it, running across the middle of the glass and, therefore, across her face. Just prior to walking out the door, Eva says to her mother, "Give me carfare, mama. I'm going to Lil's over Sunday." Her mother starts to object, but her daughter's manner is so brusque that she immediately hands over some change. Eva leaves without saying another word.

Cut to an exterior shot of the Blue Goose night club, its neon lights dancing in a circular fashion around the sign. Eva enters this high-toned establishment reluctantly and notices the smoothness of the deep carpet against the soles of her barely shod feet. She sits at a table, alone.

A singing quartet strolls from table to table, serenading the customers. When they reach Eva, one of the singers—Cabaret Charlie, naturally—recognizes her and gives her a lascivious half-grin. During the song, he caresses the girl's shoulders as she hangs her head in shame. When the quartet takes a break, Charlie sits down at her table, unbidden.

Monday night. She returns home, although her soul appears to be missing. On her feet are a shiny new pair of shoes, the very ones she had hoped for, day after day, week after week. A final title card reads: "Whatever happens, life must go on. Whatever boats are wrecked, the river does not stop flowing to the sea."

With one film, Lois Weber transformed an extra girl into a star. She believed correctly that the actress's plebian features epitomized the average American worker. More than that, Mary's sincerity comes through on the screen. Her performance in *Shoes* serves as a profound example of the subtlety that can be achieved in silent films. There is not one false note in her performance. Weber clearly impressed upon her players to act in a subdued, realistic manner, and Mary MacLaren is as disarmingly effective as the more heralded actresses of her time, including Mary Pickford, Lillian Gish, and Mae Marsh. Weber lets the camera linger on Mary's face, a face that registers pathos and longing. *Photoplay* Magazine even dubbed the tragedienne the "Sweet Sobber of Celluloid." When she was praised for her performance in *Shoes*, Mary shifted the attention to her director, saying how kind Missus Smalley had been to her.

"She put me very much at ease about the part, which is the reason I never was a bit nervous in any of the scenes. I felt every one of those scenes, and some way Missus Smalley knew exactly what to say in directing, so I was able to express the way I was sure the girl in 'Shoes' felt."

So fully did Mary immerse herself in that role that it altered her perception as an actress. "Ever since 'Shoes,'" she told Grace

Kingsley, "I have loved playing poor girls. I didn't care a bit for my elaborate dresses in 'Saving the Family Name' [1917]. My sister said I revel in rag-bags!"

With *Shoes* an unqualified success, it came as no surprise that Mary was cast as the lead in two more Weber vehicles, including one that is in sharp contrast to the director's usual fare, the comedy *The Mysterious Mrs. Musselwhite* (1917). This allowed Mary to reveal the lighter aspects of her character to her growing legion of admirers. According to *Moving Picture World*, "She is a full-fledged star in about the fastest time known to screen history."

Arriving at the studio at a specific time each day, Mary was always greeted by a particular (and favored) group of fans: a menagerie of homeless dogs. And she wouldn't think of disappointing her loyal following.

A lobby card for Douglas Fairbanks's The Three Musketeers *(1921), featuring Mary MacLaren. Author's collection.*

"I always bring some bones and things to the little 'tramp dogs' around there, and they sort of expect me," she told a writer for *Picture-Play Magazine*.

Unlike sister Katherine with her French bulldogs, Mary did not limit herself to dogs with a pedigree, not that she would ever hold that against any purebred. She was more likely to take in the sorriest-looking strays, an estimated dozen at that time. She rescued a helpless brown-and-black puppy named Heinie, who had been thrown away in a garbage can. As for Missy, she had just three legs and no one wanted her—no one but Mary that is. She was also providing for her human family. At the age of seventeen, she purchased the two-story residence at 127 North Manhattan Place in the Wilshire District of Los Angeles. This would be her home for all but a few weeks of the rest of her life.

Mary discovered some codicils in her Universal contract that she had apparently overlooked when she signed it. One was that she must obey any command given by a director. The other was that, if she should leave the studio, Universal would be in possession of the name Mary MacLaren. Not having ownership of her own name? She immediately filed a lawsuit against Universal. Needing to stay gainfully employed, she signed a three-year contract with producer David Horsley. While undergoing the stress of her legal battle, Mary suffered a concussion in a two-car collision. For a time, it was thought that she would have to undergo brain surgery. While convalescing, she sued the driver of the vehicle that hit her for $40,000. She also reached a settlement with the studio, granting her the rights to her name and an increase in pay. Dissolving the hastily made agreement with producer Horsley, Mary promptly re-signed with Universal.

By this time, the actress was strongly associated with a specific kind of role, that of a sensitive young lady who is continually wronged by the world. One such film is the now-lost drama *A Petal on the Current* (1919). Shot on location in San Francisco, it was directed by Tod Browning. He later gained a posthumous cult following for the morbid features he made starring Lon Chaney, as well as the talkies *Dracula* (1931) and *Freaks* (1932). A Mary MacLaren weeper by romance novelist Fannie Hurst seems a bit far afield for Browning, but judging by the contemporary reviews, he did well by both ladies. At least according to Universal's publicity machine, some critics speculated that Hurst had based the lead character, Stella Schump, a shy, retiring girl who works "in children's shoes at the Criterion," on Mary MacLaren's screen image.

> Stella attends a party at which she is supposed to meet a "bashful man," but he never shows. Perhaps to numb the disappointment of having been stood up, she downs her first beer, which goes straight to her head. Upon leaving the party, she strikes up a conversation with a policeman. He arrests her for public intoxication and solicitation. A night court judge sentences her to ten days in jail. She seeks outside help from her mother, to whom she writes a letter explaining her plight. Bad idea. The woman promptly keels over dead, so shocked is she by her daughter's shameful behavior. Once out of jail, Stella loses her job in the children's shoe department and finds herself broke, alone, and homeless on a park bench. Along comes a shy young fellow who finds it somehow easy to talk with this gentle girl. It turns out that he is the same bashful man she was supposed to meet at the party. The two marry and live bashfully ever after.

Just as things were finally going Mary's way, an ill wind blew into town in the form of the newly divorced Katherine. She announced that she was taking over both the family finances and the management of Mary's career. Cowed by their domineering daughter and sister, neither Lillian nor Mary nor Miriam dared object. Katherine then scheduled a face-to-face meeting with Carl Laemmle. Despite Mary's renegotiated contract, Katherine

Katherine MacDonald. Courtesy of the Media History Digital Library.

believed that her sister was *still* not being adequately compensated. When the meeting proved fruitless, Katherine insisted that Mary leave the comforting confines of Universal and branch out on her own. She also forbade Lillian from signing (for the underaged Mary) a $1 million contract with Paramount.

Despite her former status as a Manhattan socialite, Katherine deigned to try her hand at acting for the cinema. If her homely sister could be a star, just think how well *she* would do. Mary, ever accommodating, used her influence to get Katherine past the gates at Universal. An undeniably pretty girl—more conventionally so than Mary—Katherine was given the designation of the "American Beauty." But she was hardly the caliber of actress her sister was. One moviegoer opined in a letter to the editor of *Moving Picture World*: "Katherine MacDonald is beautiful but is a perfect stick when it comes to acting." Katherine wholeheartedly agreed with her harshest critics. She only cared about the million dollars she was promised by B.P. Schulberg for signing with his newly formed company, Preferred Pictures. She was given her own production unit, Katherine MacDonald Motion Pictures Corporation. Although she got away with it for a few years, audiences soon grew tired of the superficially attractive *poseur*.

Mary was still getting acting jobs, but her star had descended noticeably since leaving Universal. In addition to her supporting role in Douglas Fairbanks's *The Three Musketeers*, she was Wallace Reid's leading lady in *Across the Continent* (1922). By the time she made her final silent film, *The Dark Swan* (1924), she was billed eighth.

Seeking personal happiness, she retired from film acting to marry a British colonel, George Herbert Young, after which the couple relocated to India. Mary had nothing but good things to say about her husband: "He was so handsome," she told Richard Lamparski, "and so sweet." But India was blisteringly hot, impoverished, and living conditions were so dire that she had to leave it. Mary packed up her suitcase one day in 1928 and sailed to London, where she found work on the stage.

By 1930, Mary felt ready to return to Hollywood and resume her movie career. What she found was that during her absence from the screen, she lost what little star power she had. Like so many former silent stars, she took extra and bit parts. In all, she appeared in an estimated seventy-five sound pictures, many of which were shot at the lesser outfits on Poverty Row. Exercising her newfound interest in writing, she has a byline in a 1933 issue of *Photoplay*; the title of the article is "I Once Was a Star." Mary describes what it was like to go from being a leading lady, when the kliegs and cameras were focused on *her*, to an extra. "Now," she writes, "I am only a bit of "background, one of a hundred, one of a thousand other such, drifting unnoticed across the backdrop of the screen." She had, she added, swallowed her pride long ago. She then related an incident that clearly brought her much pain. A well-known director in the early days of talkies had once been her leading man. She had given him his start in movies, and she was willing to bet her very life on his willingness to assist her in her time of need. Not only was she desperate for a job, but she was also hungry, having eaten nothing substantial in days. Showing up, uninvited, to a party attended by many popular actors and powerful executives, she noticed the abundant refreshments that were available to the guests. She also saw her old friend. Unwilling to be seen fraternizing with some silent movie has-been, he pretended not to know her. Mary left the party, still hungry and now in tears. Hollywood's callous attitude toward those whose fortunes have ebbed has always been there, and sadly, always will be.

In the forties, Mary began taking in boarders. Her trusting, undiscerning nature was such that she took in anyone who needed a place to live, even if that individual was psychotic or sociopathic. One deeply disturbed female lodger tried to force Mary to eat poisoned pancakes. Another boarder, a man, shoved the bristle end of a broom into her eyes. Still another, the Reverend James Griffs, was a self-styled bishop, as well as a part-time hypnotist and magician. This charlatan moved in and tried to take over the rambling house with its decades of memories. Mary won a court battle and Griffs was forced to vacate the premises.

Hoping for a less perilous way to earn extra income, in July 1951, she placed an ad in the classified section of the newspaper, offering her services as a live-in companion. She had included her phone number in the ad and soon received a call. It was a promising offer made by a Mister Bickford of Beverly Hills. He told Mary that the job paid $175 per month. Room and board would also be provided at Bickford's country estate, located eighteen miles from Glendale. Interested, she invited him to her home to further discuss the matter. During the meeting, he made a critical stipulation: Mary must first submit to a "test spanking." That evening, she paid a visit to the Wilshire Police Department and swore out a complaint against Bickford. A sting operation was then hastily put into place. At an appointed time the following day, Bickford returned to Mary's residence to complete the transaction, so to speak. Little did he know that just a few feet away, hiding in a closet and observing the demeaning act, was the police sergeant. A no-doubt surprised Mister Bickford—who was actually a Glendale salesman named Robert J. Pack—was arrested and booked at the city jail on a morals charge.

Undaunted, Mary penned her first novel, *The Twisted Heart*, which tells the tale of a woman who discovers that her new husband is gay. Considered too controversial in 1952 (or perhaps it was rejected due to its dated writing style), no legitimate publisher would touch it. But Mary was determined to see the book in print; she also had high hopes of it being turned into a major motion picture. She ended up going with Exposition, a New York–based vanity press. The book's printed dedication reads:

> To my favorite living author,
> JAMES M. CAIN
> who, out of the fullness of his generous heart,
> was kind enough to edit this, my first novel.
> With profound gratitude,
> M. MacL.

Although *The Twisted Heart* was ignored at the time of publication, a rare copy of the first (and only) hardback edition turns up occasionally on eBay, selling for as much as $500. One online rare book dealer offered the following tidbit on the authoress: "Reportedly, MacLaren got additional editing help from another master of *noir* fiction, Jim Thompson, who lived with her for a time in her decrepit Hollywood mansion."

Katherine, whose movie career ended with the coming of sound, entered the cosmetics business. She may have been losing her current husband to another actress, but her boyfriend, Christian Holmes, was rich and about to get richer: he was heir to the Fleischmann's Yeast fortune. Their marriage started out well enough, with Katherine giving birth to their daughter, Ann. But less than two years later it ended with a bang when Christian shot Katherine in the shoulder during an alcohol-induced fight. In a revealing interview with Michael G. Ankerich, Ann said that her mother was exceedingly lonely following her latest divorce and attempted to fill the emptiness of her life with booze and men. Her drinking produced an ugly side to the silent screen's former American Beauty.

"Her intake," Ann said, "was nothing but skim milk and bourbon. She'd drink until she collapsed."

Seeing Mary in her "rag-bags," and hearing her prattle on about astrology, only deepened Katherine's resentment. Mary, who truly wanted to see the best in everyone, could not comprehend her sister's attitude.

"Katherine always hated me," Mary told Lamparski. "She would not let Mother sign [the $1 million contract with Paramount] for me. I don't know why because I got her into pictures and was always happy for her success. She was rich. I wasn't. But to the very end, she felt the same [antipathy] toward me."

Katherine fell victim to poor health in the 1950s. She was diagnosed with diabetes, a condition that led to the amputation of one of her legs in 1954. She then suffered several strokes, leaving her completely immobilized. She finally died, aged sixty-four, on June 4, 1956. She left a large estate, but in no way provided for her cash-strapped sister. To scrape together enough money to pay her property taxes, Mary made the painful decision to sell a prized possession: a photograph given her by Charlie Chaplin. The inscription reads: "To Mary, an old, old, old friend." It brought in $120.

Mary began to devote more time and energy to finding good homes for stray cats and dogs.

"It's a crime the way the world neglects animals," she told a reporter for the *Hollywood Citizen News*.

Mary also took in stray people. One unfortunate, a World War I veteran named Robert S. Coleman, was reported to have been beaten and robbed in his hotel room and was currently in the hospital. When Mary read his account in the newspaper, she offered him a place in her home. She admired this sad gentleman for his courage in dealing with his infirmities. The two were married in a private ceremony on February 23, 1965. During the service, the groom held Mary's gift for him: Trinka, a dog she had rescued from the pound. Coleman died six years later, in 1971.

It had been nearly two months since I received Mary's award in the mail. Every time I caught a glimpse of the wooden plaque languishing on my desk, I felt a pang of guilt. That was exacerbated by a follow-up letter from Tom Fulbright.

"In heaven's name," Tom exclaimed, "what *happened*? Are you *ill*? Have you perhaps been involved in some *horrible accident*?"

Obviously, I had put this matter off for long enough. I took a deep breath and dialed Mary MacLaren's number.

She answered on the first ring. I introduced myself and she said she had been expecting my call. My immediate impression of her was that she was cordial, completely vulnerable, and more than a bit eccentric. Naturally, I mentioned *The Three Musketeers* and told her how much I had enjoyed her performance as the Queen. I then asked her about working with the great Douglas Fairbanks.

"I absolutely *adored* Mister Fairbanks," she said. "He was so sweet."

And *that* was the extent of her film-related answers. She was much more interested in knowing my date of birth. I told her I was born on May 13. "Taurus the Bull!" she said knowingly. Astrology was more than just her hobby; it was a way of life. After gleaning additional personal information from me, she proceeded to tell me where my moon currently was, and other such ephemera. Hoping to get back to film, I asked a follow-up question, only to be told that she was a Capricorn, her birthday being January 19; she then revealed the current location of *her* moon. (Maybe I would have gotten further if I had asked about *Douglas Fairbanks's* moon.)

I mentioned that I had her award, and that I was most anxious for her to receive it. Although appreciative of Tom Fulbright's gesture, she just wasn't interested in the past; she preferred to discuss her current priorities. We talked about our respective pets, although hers outnumbered mine by a dozen to one. Still, she asked for details about our family dog, Barney. What color was he? Was he an indoor/outdoor pet? What was his astrological sign? (I may have imagined that last question.) The fact is I liked her. How could I feel any other way about someone who cared so deeply for and about animals? And she sensed in me a kindred spirit. She even invited me to come live with her full time to help care for her many strays. I thanked her for the generous offer and said I would think about it. After honestly explaining my limited options for getting the award to her, she suggested I simply put it in the mail.

"No use making a fuss," she said.

I eventually sent it, but something tells me she never quite got around to opening the package. Mary, you see, was in a perpetual state of turmoil. Her home had long been a disaster area. Clutter filled every room. There were piles of feces everywhere, and the stench of urine. Flies buzzed. Rats were in the walls. As for Mary, she slept with several dogs on a rotted mattress on the floor. Neighbors were up in arms about the condition of the property. The fire marshal viewed it as a major hazard and, in fact, the house had caught fire, leaving a hole in the roof over her bedroom. Trying to put a positive spin on it, Mary said she could see the sky from her bed.

I realize now that the last thing this courageous woman needed was a Rosemary Award. What she needed was help. Help

Mary MacLaren stands in front of the two-story home she purchased at the age of seventeen. She and the house would experience much unwelcome drama in the decades to come. Courtesy of silentsaregolden.com.

with finances. Help for her animals. Help hauling away garbage and humanely ridding the area of vermin. She needed a decent meal and a bath. A literal roof over her head. The Los Angeles County officials offered no such assistance; instead, they hounded her with fines and threatened her with legal action. With no one to defend her but herself, she convinced the Superior Court commissioner that she was competent. But the county was persistent, and eighty-five-year-old Mary was outnumbered. There came that sad day when she was escorted out of her home of nearly seventy years and placed in a West Hollywood nursing facility. The house was sold at auction, with the proceeds going to the state. The dogs and cats—Mary's family—went to the pound. As for Mary, she would live for just a few more weeks. Without her home, her very identity, without her babies, what was her purpose in life? There was no anger, no bitterness. She cooperated with the staff and was, according to one of her caregivers, "a lovely, lovely, lovely lady, just as sweet as she could be."

Four

Bob Chatterton: Underfoot in Hollywood

Courtesy of the Wisconsin Center for Film and Theatre Research.

I love Laurel & Hardy. So, when I read that a retrospective of their films was to be held at the Unicorn Theatre, an art house in La Jolla, I made a point of attending. The presenter, a heavyset sixty-year-old man named Bob Chatterton, showed some rare (for the time) film clips, interspersed with background information. What made this program unique was that the host had personally known both Stan Laurel and Oliver Hardy.

Around the halfway point of his presentation, he announced to the handful of people in the audience that he needed to attend to his two elderly dachshunds, who were waiting patiently in the back seat of his car, but that he would return shortly. He then stood up and, with his ultra-serious expression in place, slowly made his way up the aisle of the auditorium. I found his devotion to his canine friends heartwarming. It was also plain to see that this was someone afflicted. When he walked, one foot turned out, the result of his having polio as a child. I know this because, after the program, I spent quite a while talking with him. Bob Chatterton, I soon realized, was an interesting person, one who loved film as much as I.

That love began in the early 1940s. He became the curator of the Memorable Films Society in Cleveland, Ohio, where he was born in 1918. This led to Bob moving to Hollywood, his bailiwick for the rest of his life. During World War II, he directed productions at the Hollywood Canteen Playhouse, where volunteers performed musicals for members of the armed forces. Postwar, he served as director of the Hollywood Playhouse Workshop. From 1944 through 1948, he worked as a freelance writer and actor. During that period he also headed the Cinema Arts Society and was employed at the Old-Time Movie Theatre, the Nickelodeon, and was a film booker for the Co-operative Theatres chain in Los Angeles. He also taught occasional courses in motion picture appreciation and made appearances on several television talk shows. This allowed him to meet, and occasionally befriend, some of Hollywood's biggest names. He counted among his acquaintances Judy Garland and her second husband Sid Luft, and Madame Sul-Te-Wan, the pioneering black actress who had appeared in *The Birth of a Nation* (1915). In 1967, he began presenting his "Film Chats" at various universities and film societies across the country. Each program was approximately two hours in length, with the film portion occupying about ninety minutes. These "illustrated lectures," which included exclusive footage from Bob's personal collection, covered a variety of topics, including individual screen personalities, musical highlights, silent, and underground films. In all, he assembled thirty-four separate programs, an impressive achievement.

Bob was also something of a shutterbug. In 1948, he shot 16mm footage of D.W. Griffith's funeral in Hollywood. Charlie Chaplin, Mack Sennett, and Erich Von Stroheim were among the mourners he captured on film. He also photographed Laurel & Hardy's

Stan Laurel and Oliver Hardy strike characteristic poses for a publicity shoot at 20th Century-Fox, in 1944. Photo courtesy of Jerry Murbach (doctormacro.com).

final joint appearance on camera in 1956. In 1961, he shot footage of Stan alone in the retired comedian's Santa Monica apartment. Stan is in especially good humor as he manipulates a pair of Laurel & Hardy marionettes; he also proudly shows off his recently received Oscar, an honor he shared with his late partner.

Stan Laurel—born Arthur Stanley Jefferson in Ulverston, England, on June 16, 1890—and Oliver Norvell "Babe" Hardy—born in Harlem, Georgia, on January 18, 1892—had each been in the movie business for some time before they were employed at the Hal Roach Studios in Culver City, California. Supervising director Leo McCarey was the one who saw their potential as a team. In 1927, Laurel & Hardy made their official debut in a prison escape picture called *The Second Hundred Years*. By the following year they had become the public's favorite comedy duo. They made a seamless transition to sound films and their popularity continued to grow, not only in the United States but around the world. Their childlike characters, Stanley and Ollie, depended solely on each other in an often hostile world. So endearing were they that it didn't matter what language they were speaking. Oliver Hardy was a fine actor who spent his off hours on the Lakeside Country Club golf course or at the Santa Anita racetrack. Stan, who had celluloid in his blood, was the guiding creative force behind their comedies. He worked in tandem with the writers, cameramen, lighting technicians, directors, and editors to produce what were (and remain) among the finest comedies ever produced. One of their best-known films, *The Music Box*, has the Boys as professional moving men who are hired to deliver a crated player piano up a long flight of stairs to a house located "right on top of the stoop." This three-reel exercise in comic frustration earned the team and their producer, Hal Roach, an Academy Award for Best Short Subject of 1932. In all, Stan and Babe would make 107 films together: thirty-two silent shorts, forty sound shorts, twenty-three features, and twelve guest appearances. Their final film, a French-Italian-American production called *Atoll K*, was released in 1951. They also toured the music halls with a live show, in England, Ireland, Wales, and Scotland. While on these late-career tours, Stan and Babe became close personal friends.

In 1954, the comedians were genuinely floored to be the subjects of Ralph Edwards's television program *This is Your Life*. Although Stan took part in the show, he made it clear that he was not happy that he and his partner would be appearing live on network television with neither rehearsal nor remuneration. He did receive a parting gift of a kinescope of their episode and a 16mm sound projector. He immediately turned the projector over to Bob, who recalled that it sounded like a coffee grinder when it was running. Stan watched the film over and over, criticizing what he considered his and Babe's performances. According to the many letters he received from members of the public, the show was greatly enjoyed by fans who theretofore knew little about the team's history. Far more detrimental to their careers than an unplanned television appearance was Babe Hardy's faltering health. Then sixty-three and weighing at least 350 pounds, he suffered a heart attack, his second. His doctor put him on a low-cholesterol diet, causing him to lose 150 pounds within a few months' time.

Stan's daughter, Lois Jr., invited her father and Babe, along with their respective wives, Ida and Lucille, to a Sunday afternoon barbecue at her home in Tarzana in 1956. Stan brought along a teenaged fan named Andy Wade. Andy and his father, residents of Florida, made the long drive to California each summer, just so the young man could spend time with Stan. Bob also claimed to have been present, movie camera in hand. Stan, ever the perfectionist, made it clear that any footage taken that day was to be kept strictly private. Bob and Andy agreed to this. Stan was therefore distressed when those few minutes of color footage began turning up for sale in 8mm prints bearing the incongruous title, "Stan Visits Ollie." Since that time, it has been widely circulated and used in various documentaries. The original 16mm print has recently been restored and digitized for inclusion on the CineMuseum Blu-ray set *Stooge O-Rama* (2023). The backyard in the film looks like countless other suburban backyards of average Americans in the 1950s. Ida and Lucille appear briefly, posing self-consciously on Lois's driveway. Stan, seated at the picnic table and painfully aware of the camera, smokes incessantly. At one point he is seen walking a short distance, limping as a result of a recent stroke. The shot that generates the biggest reaction is of Stan and Babe together. Babe is dramatically thinner than he had been in recent years. Because he is not wearing a necktie, he twiddles Stan's instead. The film as a whole is rather bleak, despite the forced gaiety of all involved. Andy Wade momentarily steps in between the two icons and they both gleefully point at him. Another sad aspect of this film is that the teenaged Andy died prematurely, in 1960.

Despite his best efforts, Babe's health continued to decline. He died, aged sixty-five, on August 7, 1957. Stan was devastated. He never acted in another film, not even when Stanley Kramer offered him a well-compensated cameo role in the comic extravaganza *It's a Mad, Mad, Mad, Mad World* (1963), which featured a host of old-time comedians. He also declined Jerry Lewis's offer to devise gags for his then-popular comedies. The one concession Stan made to his past career was writing new Laurel & Hardy gags and sketches that would never be performed. He said it made him feel closer to Babe. Stan, a diabetic and the victim of several strokes, was in poor health for many years. He passed away, at the age of seventy-four, on February 23, 1965. Bob deeply mourned the loss of his friend.

Film collectors in the seventies fell into two distinct groups: those who restricted themselves to the legal avenue by purchasing prints from the Blackhawk and Castle Films catalogues, and those who sought out and obtained (through often complicated, and sometimes questionable, means) whatever print their heart desired. Bob was most definitely in the latter group. This proved risky at the time, as Roddy McDowall would have attested. In 1975, the FBI raided the actor's home and confiscated his prized film collection, the majority of which was still protected by copyright. In his many years on the Hollywood scene, Bob had acquired every kind of film imaginable, from beautiful reduction prints of his favorite 1940s musicals to more raunchy fare. If you wanted to make a gonzo film collector uneasy, all you had to say was, "So, tell me, where did you get that print?" Due to the sheer rarity of Bob's films, fellow aficionados eagerly attended his "Parlour Cinema" evenings in the living room of his low-ceilinged bungalow in North Hollywood, beginning in the late sixties. Several noted film historians were regular attendees, including DeWitt Bodeen, Anthony Slide, and Robert Osborne (later the on-camera host on the Turner Classic Movies network). Richard Lamparski, who attended during his frequent trips to the West Coast, later wrote about these memorable screenings in his memoir *Hollywood Diary* (BearManor Media, 2006). According to Lamparski, Bob's rules for these gatherings were strictly enforced.

1. No smoking.
2. No talking once the projector begins to roll, and no comments that could be considered criticism or ridicule, no matter what is on the screen.
3. Use the john before or after each feature only.
4. If you use a folding chair, collapse it and return it to the corner before leaving.
5. On your way out, place two dollars in the cigar box by the door.

There were two things Bob Chatterton wanted all Parlour Cinema newcomers to know from the outset. One was that he was related to the versatile stage and screen actress Ruth Chatterton (1892–1961), who had twice been nominated for an Academy Award. She was Bob's father's first cousin. The other bit of information was that in the parking lot on the left of his apartment building once stood the home of world-heavyweight boxing champion Jack Dempsey. Lamparski later found a twenties-era souvenir postcard of that house and sent it to Bob for Christmas. He proudly framed it and hung it in his bathroom.

Sometimes, a celebrity would be one of Bob's special guests. Mae Clarke (the actress who got a grapefruit to the face courtesy of James Cagney in the crime drama *The Public Enemy*) showed up to watch an exceptional print of another of her pictures from 1931, *Waterloo Bridge*. Judy Canova was there for a double feature of her Republic B-movie comedies. In December 1970, Bob hosted a special showing of the 1944 MGM musical, *Meet Me in St. Louis*, directed by Vincente Minnelli and starring Judy Garland. The bland juvenile lead about whom Judy sings "The Boy Next Door" was Tom Drake, that evening's guest of honor. The former actor, now fifty-one and wearing an unconvincing toupée, had fallen on lean times. Like so many in his uncertain profession, he had struggled with alcoholism. His then-current job as a used car salesman (in a lot practically across the street from his former studio) was the best he could do while waiting for his acting career to get back on track. Shy of people, Drake arrived early at Bob's place and sequestered himself in the host's bedroom until just prior to the start of the picture. When the lights came back on nearly two hours later, Tom was applauded and generally fawned over, Hollywood style. Everybody there asked him endless questions about Judy, who by then was known and loved as a gay icon. One guest was hardly as impressed—or polite.

"*You're* Tom Drake?" he said in disbelief. "I would *never* have recognized you from what we saw tonight. What *happened* to you?"

When putting together a letter to me, Bob apparently spent several hours going through old magazines and cutting out words and pictures. He would then construct his missive using these printed images. Every time I got one of his pasted-up letters in the mail, I felt like I was reading a ransom note. But it gave Bob something to do with his time. The fact is the man was terribly lonely. He had many acquaintances but few actual friends. Because of his need for company, one of his letters to me included an invitation to stay the weekend at his house. I RSVP'd in the affirmative.

It just so happened that my sister Cynthia and her husband Larry were going to a wedding in L.A. on the weekend in question. I asked if I could tag along and be dropped off at Bob's chosen meeting place, the parking lot of the Variety Arts Club, of which he was a longtime member. I packed an overnight bag and was ready to go. As we arrived at our destination, on Figueroa Street in downtown Los Angeles, my protective sister did not like the look of the rundown neighborhood. She began to point out some of the undesirable citizens who were out and about that morning. "I don't know about this," she said. "I mean, look at that guy over there—he looks like a convict."

"*That's* the guy I'm staying with," I said.

"Oh, he doesn't look *that* bad," she said, back peddling as gracefully as possible.

Less than a minute later, I was greeting my host.

"Hi, Bob. You look terrible." (That was me at nineteen: a total smartass.)

"Thank you," Bob replied with his deadpan delivery.

Since we were already there, Bob asked if I wanted to take a tour of the Variety Arts Club, housed in a five-story Italian-Renaissance-inspired building dating back to 1924.

"Lead on, my good man," I said.

It was a fascinating place for someone of my ilk, a veritable warehouse of show business memorabilia, its walls covered with framed movie posters and signed celebrity portraits. One was of Ed Wynn, "The Perfect Fool," prompting me to launch into my impression of him. There was even an old-fashioned card catalogue containing Milton Berle's legendary joke file, although I read a few of them and they hadn't aged too well. Bob booked various acts to appear at the club. The following year, in fact, he presented British chanteuse (and star of 1934's *Evergreen*) Jessie Matthews in her one-woman show.

After the tour, Bob and I were on our way to his home, which was in a sketchy neighborhood, as evidenced by the iron bars on the windows. We were greeted by the cheerful barking of his dachshunds and the chirping of his green parakeet, Billy Bitzer. To freshen up after the long drive, I excused myself to use the bathroom. From the vantage point of the toilet was a photo of Marie Dressler, staring disapprovingly at the viewer. Next to that was a Playgirl calendar, featuring Mister June in all his glory.

Good God, *what* had I gotten myself into?

I must have had a chip on my shoulder because Bob commented on my change in mood. I told him I had just seen Mister June and that it made me uncomfortable.

Poor Bob: he started to cry. "I open my heart to you, and you don't accept me," he said sadly. "You know, being friends with someone means you can talk about more than just Laurel & Hardy."

I felt terrible. Here I was, a guest in this nice man's home, and I was overtly judging him. Granted, 1978 was a far less enlightened time, but that didn't excuse my behavior. I sincerely apologized and Bob was quick to forgive me. The subject of his lifestyle would enter our conversations a few more times during that visit, but I was better prepared for it. One of the things he told me was that he was, despite being in his sixties, still quite active sexually. Being on the thick side, he attracted a subset of gay men known as "chubby chasers." Call me naïve, but this was all new to me. When Bob and I paid a visit to the Burbank home of his sister, Jean Cash, who took care of their ninety-seven-year-old mother, there was a visitor, a well-dressed, well-spoken Asian man in his mid-to-late thirties. When I asked about the nature of his relationship to the Chatterton family, Bob, Jean, and the guest laughed knowingly.

"Just a good friend," the man said.

He was, Bob told me later, a chubby chaser.

Another such reference dealt with Bob's experience as an avant-garde filmmaker in the early sixties. He showed me one of his mildly risqué movies, which was shot silent and in color at Venice Beach. It features a flamboyantly effeminate man (Taylor Mead) who spends the bulk of the thirty-two-minute film pursuing a butch fisherman who is only interested in fishing. It is called

Passion in a Seaside Slum, and it all seemed rather silly to me. Bob told me that he had screened it for Stan and Ida Laurel at their apartment. Ida (or Eda, as Stan spelled it), a Russian with a bawdy sense of humor, laughed uproariously throughout. Stan, who could seemingly find humor in any situation, didn't smile even once. When The End title appeared, Stan turned to Bob and said, "Shocking, Bob. Absolutely shocking." And that was the extent of his review. However, during Bob's next visit, Stan said, "About your film: it really *is* very funny." But he *still* never cracked a smile. As slight as *Passion in a Seaside Slum* is, it has attained a level of respectability under the heading of pioneering LGBTQ+ films. I recently read online that it has been preserved by Anthology Film Archives and Los Angeles Film Forum through the Avante-Garde masters grant program founded by the Film Foundation. I may not have cared for the film, but I'm glad that Bob's effort has not been forgotten.

Before going out for lunch, Bob took me to a few of his neighbors' homes for quick visits. I was reminded of the unfortunate characters in Nathanael West's novel *The Day of the Locust*. One was Coit, an obese gay man who lived a few doors away from Bob's house. Coit had apparently been a child actor in the thirties ("a movie moppet" was Bob's description) but was now an agoraphobic recluse. Bob then took me to Gale Sondergaard's modest abode (there were bars on her windows as well), but, unfortunately, she wasn't at home. I would love to have complimented her on her Mrs. Danvers-like performance in the 1946 Abbott & Costello film *The Time of Their Lives*.

Lunch was greasy burgers and Cokes at a hole-in-the-wall diner on Hollywood Boulevard. At least we didn't eat at what may well have been the world's least appetizing restaurant, one that attempted to entice passersby with a window display featuring plates of dusty plastic food. At that time, the world-famous thoroughfare was a depressing example of urban decay. The Hollywood Walk of Fame, with its inlaid stars featuring the names of motion picture notables, was grimy with neglect. Tacky shops sold tacky souvenirs. The Hollywood Wax Museum charged customers to see mannequins that bore scant resemblance to their movie star subjects. Other establishments were meant to appeal to more prurient interests. Frederick's of Hollywood, a trashy lingerie supplier, displayed a sampling of its immodest wares in the flagship store's front window. Prostitutes of all ages and genders leaned against graffiti-covered walls, awaiting their next Johns. There was the Pussycat Theatre, its marquee boldly proclaiming the lurid titles of that week's XXX-rated pornographic films. A genuine landmark dating back to 1927, the pagoda-themed Grauman's Chinese Theatre was now *Mann's* Chinese Theatre, renamed after the latest owner, Ted Mann. The famed HOLLYWOOD sign, with its forty-five-foot-tall white letters that had been erected in 1923, was in such a state of deterioration that it would be taken down within a matter of weeks, leaving the hills bare for three months. It took a fundraiser by Hugh Hefner at the Playboy mansion to pay for its replacement. "This town," the publishing mogul said, "never had a good sense of its own history."[1]

Bob made occasional references to his memoir-in-progress, of which he only wrote the title: "Underfoot in Hollywood." It's a shame that he didn't leave a written record of his experiences. Bob knew every street where seemingly every film had been shot. After lunch, he took me on a driving tour of the movies' most significant locations—at least the most significant to *me*. Bear in mind, this was long before there were plaques designating them as historic landmarks.

The Mack Sennett Company was once a fixture in Echo Park, and nearby public streets had routinely been used by Del Lord, Sennett's top director in the twenties, for chase scenes featuring the Keystone Kops and others. One especially hilly street, Scott

---

[1] Hollywood history is far more celebrated in the 2020s than it was in the 1970s; the $50 million Academy Museum of Motion Pictures is a prime example. The HOLLYWOOD sign was refurbished again in 2010. As for Mann's Chinese Theatre, it reverted to its original name in 2013.

Avenue, would be revisited by the director in 1935, when he was working for the Columbia Short Subjects Department. This was for the Three Stooges' two-reeler *Three Little Beers*. I could almost see the beer barrels rolling down that hill as they had in the film, made forty-three years earlier. We then stopped in front of another choice location: an absurdly long (and steep) stairway in the Silver Lake district, at 2212 Edendale Place. I first thought we were looking at the famous steps used in Laurel & Hardy's *The Music Box* as well as their earlier, and currently "lost," silent two-reeler *Hats Off!* (1927). *Those* steps, Bob informed me, were on Vendome Street. *These* steps (all 147 of them) were the setting for another of my favorite Stooge shorts, *An Ache in Every Stake* (1941), also directed by Del Lord, when he still had a big enough budget to shoot exteriors. Seeing these sites in person was a joy, but the one that truly inspired a sense of awe was the former location, at 4500 Sunset, at the junction of Hollywood Boulevard and Silver Lake. That, Bob told me, is where D.W. Griffith built his mammoth set for *Intolerance* (1916), depicting Babylon, circa 539 B.C., with its rearing sculpted elephants atop 300-foot-tall towers. I respectfully bowed my head while standing before the supermarket that stands (at least partially) in its place. Bob was pleased by my strong reaction to this little-known form of Hollywood detective work.[2]

Our next stop was the padlocked storage unit where Bob kept his film collection. He told me to pick out anything I wanted to see. Talk about being the proverbial kid in the candy store! Of course, our time was limited, but Bob assured me I could (and should) visit him again, and very soon. Reading the carefully labeled titles on the sides of the cans, I was struck by the large number of classic films in my friend's collection.

---

2 Bob would have been gratified had he lived to read the three fascinating books on silent movie locations written by my good friend John Bengtson, *Silent Echoes: Buster Keaton; Silent Traces: Charlie Chaplin;* and *Silent Visions: Harold Lloyd* (Santa Monica Press, 2000, 2006, and 2011, respectively.)

Babylon is erected on Sunset Boulevard, Los Angeles, 1916. Courtesy of John Bengtson.

Babylon, 539 B.C. as imagined by the Father of Film D.W. Griffith, for Intolerance (1916). Courtesy of the Museum of Modern Art Film Stills Archive.

The Three Stooges prepare to deliver blocks of ice up a long flight of stairs. An Ache in Every Stake (1941). © Columbia Pictures.

The same steps, decades later. Photo by John Bengtson.

"Do you ever worry about fires, Bob?" I asked. "I mean, what would you do if these were destroyed?"

He merely shrugged and said, "They're just things; it's not like they're people or animals."

Later that day, we watched several films, the majority of which were comedies. When something struck me as funny, I would laugh out loud. When I did, Bob would give me one of his rare smiles. It obviously delighted him to be sharing his films with someone who appreciated them.

Bob was a gracious host. He was always preparing snacks for us, including JELL-O vanilla pudding with freshly sliced bananas. Bob loved sweets. He didn't ask me what I wanted, he would just stand silently in the kitchen with an old-fashioned hand mixer and put something together. Carrying two bowls over to the sofa, he wordlessly handed one to me and kept the other for himself. That night, I slept with the dachshunds on that same couch, something I could never have done in my parents' house, with their "no dogs allowed" policy.

The following day, as I was preparing to be picked up and driven home by my wedding-going sister and brother-in-law, Bob handed me an odd-looking trinket. It was, he said, Stan's favorite ashtray. Approximately four inches long, it has a finger-ring handle that is connected to a lacquered reddish-orange bowl, two inches in diameter and approximately one-half-inch deep. A screw which held the piece together had come loose, and Stan fixed it by using a different-sized screw in its place. Because this ashtray could not accommodate more than a couple of cigarette butts, Stan relegated it to the bathroom. I thanked him, although I didn't know what to make of the item itself. As there was no provenance, I had to take Bob's word that his backstory was true, and because he could be something of a fabulist, I was reticent to believe everything he said.

Bob's diabetes, exacerbated by his escalating weight and addiction to sweets, began to take its toll on his overall health.

One year, he didn't get his outdoor holiday lights put up until the day *after* Christmas. I kept in touch with him, but never to his satisfaction. At one point, he wrote to say that, had he known our friendship would fade, he would *never* have gifted me with Stan's ashtray. I didn't know how to respond to that. I couldn't send it back; that would be rude. So, I sat down and wrote a note saying just how much that personal gift meant to me. Privately, however, I was looking for an exit strategy. If there's one thing that sours me on a relationship, it's guilt. God knows, I carry around enough guilt for an entire Catholic family, extended relatives included.

At the beginning of 1986, my annual Christmas card to Bob was returned, marked "Deceased." It turns out that he had died in his home the previous year, on Thursday, April 25, at the age of sixty-seven. I felt that I had failed him. So much so, that every time I saw that ashtray, I felt uneasy. Deb and I discussed this and, after thinking about it for a while, she suggested I send it to the eminent author John McCabe, who had written four books on Stan and Babe, including the affectionate dual-biography, *Mr. Laurel & Mr. Hardy* (Doubleday, 1961). In his response, Prof. McCabe confirmed that the item had indeed belonged to Stan, and that he was very grateful to have it.

And with that one appreciative sentence, my conflict disappeared.

FIVE
Eddie LeVeque: The Last of the Keystone Kops

Courtesy of the Media History Digital Library.

When discussing film history, it is generally wise to steer clear of "firsts." You know: the first closeup, the first story-driven film, the first blockbuster. As soon as someone labels something as a first, someone else comes along with an earlier example of it. It never fails.

The same can be true of "lasts": the last Civil War veteran, the last survivor of the *Titanic*, the last person to own a flip phone. As I write this, there is only one documented survivor of the silent era. His name is Garry Watson, and he was born on September 27, 1928. Garry is the last surviving member of the nine Watson siblings, known as "Hollywood's First Family." So, I guess you can say he's both a first *and* a last.

For a time in the early 1970s, there seemed to be a competition for the title of The Last Keystone Kop. This mattered because even those who know next to nothing about silent movies have heard of the Kops—that antiquated group of bumbling policemen, running in circles with their billy clubs aloft, chasing the bad guys they never seem to catch. Even those who have never seen Mack Sennett's finest in action have heard sports or political commentators pejoratively describe a team or members of Congress as "acting like Keystone Kops." I was privileged to know a couple of the original members of that band of merry lawmen, those who appeared in the films made at Keystone from 1912 to 1917. One was Robert Cox (1895–1974), whom I wrote about in our book *CHASE!* The other was Eddie LeVeque. On a weekday afternoon in 1980, I found Eddie's name in the Greater Los Angeles phone book and dialed the number. He answered immediately.

"Am I speaking to the Last of the Keystone Kops?"

He chuckled and said, "That you are, sir. And who am I speaking to, please?"

I introduced myself and explained that I was a longtime silent film buff. I then asked if he would mind answering a few questions about his days at Keystone and beyond.

"Ask me anything you wish, sir."

I liked this man already. He was so pleasant, and his soft voice had more than a hint of old Mexico in it. Having never seen a photo of Eddie, I tried to imagine what he looked like. That was answered for me by another writer, Walter Wagner, who had met him in 1973.

> He is the compleat Keystone Kop. Bulbous-nosed; a winking smile; laughing, upturned, bushy eyebrows; a round arc of a face with blue eyes that glint merrily and mischievously, especially when he talks about the unforgotten, zany antics of the screen's wildest police force.

"Let's begin at the beginning," I said. "Where were you born, and when?"

As someone accustomed to giving interviews, he had his answers at the ready. He told me that he was born in Juarez, Mexico, on June 4, 1896. From the beginning, show business was in Eddie's blood. His maternal granduncle, Rito Armendariz, whom he described as "the black sheep of the family," was a versatile entertainer. Combining his talents as a puppeteer, a mime, a clown, a writer, and a singer, he put on shows for the local children. Beginning at age four, Eddie was put to work in these productions, often cast as a little girl. At seven, he was given his parents' permission to go on the road with Uncle Rito, performing in towns big and small, in Mexico, Texas, and Arizona. A major addition to the act in 1904 were moving pictures. While Eddie turned the crank on Rito's newly acquired Edison projector, the spectators gazed with rapt attention at the images being projected onto a suspended white sheet. This became their window into other worlds. Ocean waves silently pounded the shore. A grizzled-looking cowboy fired his pistol directly at the viewer. A belly dancer from Tombstone, Arizona, billed as

Little Egypt, undulated suggestively, causing some mothers in the audience to cover their innocent sons' eyes. Eddie especially enjoyed the French films of the Pathé Frères, featuring frenetic gendarmes chasing a crook through the narrow streets of Paris.

The nomadic lifestyle was an exciting one for young Eddie. He would always cherish the memories of hopping freight and passenger trains, traveling from stop to stop without paying a peso. It must have been wearying, however, for his aging uncle. Three years after setting out on the road together, Rito passed away, bringing their adventure to an abrupt end.

Returning home to El Paso, Eddie had another tragedy to face. His father, Edward LeVeque Sr., a French gentleman gambler from New Orleans, often carried large amounts of cash, which put him at risk of robbery. In 1906, he was attacked by two assailants with sandbags, fracturing his skull. For two years he lingered. It was a merciful release when he finally succumbed to his injuries. Eddie's mother, a Mexican from Chihuahua, was now a widow and, as such, she needed her son to stay close to home. For several years, he suppressed his wanderlust.

While staying at the El Paso YMCA in 1911, Eddie met a cameraman from the Pathé News. His name was Lewis, although Eddie never knew for certain if that was his first or last name. Filming live events for newsreels was becoming a lucrative business, and Lewis explained that he was going into Mexico to shoot footage of the Madero Revolution, and he needed an assistant. The pay, he said, was one American dollar a day. Eddie was in, and the pair of itinerant filmmakers shot every battle they could find. When none were occurring, they would round up as many soldiers as possible and fake it. The soldiers proved to be adept actors, taking Lewis's direction (with Eddie interpreting for him) and putting everything they had into the ersatz battle scenes. Audiences never knew the difference.

Edward LeVeque, age six, June 1902. Courtesy of Michael Campino.

An offer to work for the Selig Polyscope Company in Chicago did not bear fruit, but an application to the American Film Company did. Eddie had a letter of recommendation from Lewis, which touted his skills as a projectionist, cameraman, actor, and assistant director. He was hired on the spot. Eddie had this to say about that primitive era of film.

In those days anyone who had the slightest bit of experience with a camera could usually get work at a studio. The industry was in its infancy. I was hired at ten dollars a week and played bits in half- and one-reelers …. The directors at American had all come from the stage, and they directed movies like they were plays. They understood nothing of the fluidity of the camera. The actors, four or five of us, would move toward the camera. That was the close-up. The camera never moved toward the actors.

When the American Film Company relocated to California, Eddie was not invited to come along. So, he went home to El Paso again, where he met General Pancho Villa (1878–1923). One of Eddie's friends was employed by Villa as his chauffeur; it was he who introduced Eddie to the general, who was in the market for an interpreter. Eddie got the job, although it was not to his liking. He was amazed by Villa's insatiable hunger for publicity, "worse than any movie star," he said. What really distressed him was the realization that he was working for a terrorist, a thief, and a rapist. Slipping out of Villa's camp, he walked the sixty miles to El Paso.

Eddie decided to leave Texas—for good this time—and find work in moving pictures. He got a job on a passenger train as a news butcher, selling papers, magazines, books, postcards, and Indian beadwork. When he arrived at his destination, he soon understood why Hollywood was referred to as "the most beautiful suburb in America." The weather was warm and sunny, even in the winter months. Lemon, orange, and walnut groves flourished, and the streets were lined with shady pepper trees. This was the playground for an industry that had grown from an impulsive experiment to a thriving business—and Eddie was thrilled to be a part of it. His first job was as one of the thousands of extras in several scenes of the three-and-a-half-hour epic *Intolerance* (1916).

Eddie next applied for work at the Keystone Film Company, located at 1712 Allesandro Boulevard in Edendale.[3] Established in 1912, the Keystone Film Company was overseen by Mack Sennett. Born Michael Sinnott in Quebec, Canada, on January 17, 1880, he grew up very poor, working in a boiler factory. In 1908, he was hired as an actor by the American Biograph Company in New York City, under the direction of D.W. Griffith. In 1909, the director allowed his protégé to star in *The Curtain Pole*, an Americanized version of a French chase comedy.

Sennett received the financial backing of producers Adam Kessel and Charles Baumann and relocated to California. The Keystone Film Company earned a solid reputation as purveyors of slapstick comedies. Sennett was a rough-hewn Irishman, a tough boss, a coarse individual (stories of his careless use of a spittoon are legendary), and a genius when it came to discovering new comic talent. Over the years he made stars out of Mabel Normand, Charlie Chaplin, Roscoe Arbuckle, Gloria Swanson,

---

3 Edendale is an historical name for a district northeast of downtown Los Angeles, in what is currently known as Echo Park, Los Feliz, and Silver Lake.

Mack Swain, Marie Prevost, Phyllis Haver, Harry Langdon, and others. Sennett's inability to pay his principals what they were worth caused them to leave for greener pastures.

It was eight thirty in the morning when Eddie first walked into Harry Atkinson's office. Getting his attention, Eddie began to reel off his qualifications, producing some photographs as evidence. Atkinson was impressed with a shot of Eddie posing with the notorious Pancho Villa. Mentioning this to Charles Avery, the director said, "I could use a new prop boy."

"From prop boy I graduated to doubling for girls," Eddie laughed. "When one of the female stars on the lot couldn't do a stunt or a fall, I'd put on a dress and do it for her, things like jumping from a speeding automobile or trolley car .... I was agile and it came easy for me."

The stunt work was followed by bit parts, sometimes as a Kop. But then, virtually every actor on the Keystone payroll wore the familiar uniform at one time or another. Eddie had not forgotten the French gendarme pictures he and his uncle screened in their traveling show. Those had been the forerunner to Sennett's creation.

"What Sennett added," Eddie said, "was putting the Kops in automobiles."

The earliest pictures in which the Kops appear are rather dusty affairs, shot outdoors, made up on the spot, and played to the hilt with a rustic sense of humor. In *Bangville Police*, released in April 1913, they wear plain, farm-style overalls. By the time they barged their way into *A Muddy Romance* in November of that year, they had found their trademark look: old-fashioned (even for the time) police uniforms with long coats and brass buttons, loose-fitting trousers, and tall, rounded (and slightly dented) grey helmets. Sennett, who could never resist a bargain, had purchased the lot of discarded uniforms from the LAPD, which had traded in those helmets for the sleeker-looking black caps. By 1915, the Keystone Kops had done the same.

"Sennett ... tried to call us the Mack Sennett Kops, but the public gave us our name," Eddie insisted. "The Keystone name was very famous then, and people just started calling us the Keystone Kops. Despite Sennett's displeasure, the name stuck. All the other studios tried to copy the Keystone Kops. There were the Universal Cops, the Stern Brothers Cops, the Christie Cops, and the [Fox] Sunshine Cops. But they never had the popularity of the Keystone Kops."

Eddie was not exaggerating; audiences really did love them. The point of the Keystone comedies—whether in half, single, or double reels—was to make moviegoers laugh. Many of the patrons frequenting the nickelodeons were immigrants—hardworking men and women willing to spend a nickel on some much-needed laughter. Creating that laughter was no easy task. The men who played the Keystone Kops literally risked their lives to make those early action films. Eddie said that the only direction he remembered the team receiving was: "All right, boys, do what you want, do what's funny, only don't hurt yourselves." Of course, when it's time to fall out of the paddy wagon or jump into the Pacific from a high pier, such a warning doesn't count for much. There were injuries. In some cases, not many thankfully, a Keystone employee would be killed while attempting a dangerous stunt. No wonder people routinely said to Eddie, "You must be crazy to work at Keystone. That's a nut place, a crazy factory." When asked why he stayed, the only answer would be: "Three dollars a day."

Eddie had one story that shows just how hazardous a Kop's life could be. The scene involves a shack that has been set afire. The doorway is blocked by a piano, of all things, making an escape impossible for the Kop—in this case, Eddie—stuck inside the shack. Although the piano is supposed to be a breakaway, it refuses to break. The fire intensifies and Eddie begins to fear for his life. He screams to be let out. His fellow Kops, understanding the gravity of the situation, use axes to break apart the piano, thus allowing their colleague's escape. He is safe, but worse for the wear. And the scene stays in the picture.

To knowingly put himself in harm's way, Eddie employed a type of self-hypnosis.

Once we were in the car and the chase began, you forgot yourself and you just took chances. I took many a fall that was unnecessary, but [every Kop] was trying to outdo everyone else. There was always the spirit of good-natured competition. The only thing that mattered was to make it look funny. On the screen it looked like we were traveling, *zooosh*, a hundred miles an hour! We were going about forty, which was still dangerous when you leaped from a moving car. The fast chases were trick photography.

By that, he meant the camera would be cranked at half-speed, known in the trade as undercranking, creating a fast-motion effect. This trick was vital to the appeal of the Kops. With practically everyone in the country owning a Model T Ford, speed was king. Keystone's directors used the streets of Los Angeles to stage some breathtaking car chases. The filmmakers started very early in the morning to avoid outside interference. In preparation for those death-defying skids and spins, actual city streets were doused with oil to ensure the most slippery surface possible. The director carefully explained the maneuvers he wanted the actors and stunt doubles to perform—and then let the cameras roll. The filmmakers were back at the studio, editing the footage, before the shopkeepers and police could discover the oil-soaked streets. This messy substance was later abandoned in favor of washable soap.

Eddie had earned his place on the force. He was even given a nickname: "Mex."

The fellows at Keystone used to kid me about my English, and the more they kidded me the more mistakes I made. It had been the same at the American Film Company. Eddie Gribbon took me under his wing and helped correct my English. Jack Dillon, Eddie Cline, Charley Avery, Harry Atkinson, and others took a liking to me since I used to show them the best places to eat good Mexican and Spanish food, as well as helping them meet handsome Mexican señoritas of the upper classes, refugees of the revolution.

In 1917, Sennett gave up the Keystone moniker and began producing two-reelers under his own name. The Mack Sennett Comedies were a vast improvement, both creatively and technically, on the often-slapdash Keystones. The Kops would turn up occasionally in the two-reelers of the twenties, bearing little resemblance to their earlier incarnations. Their uniforms were now sleek, modern, and correctly sized. No longer the jumping maniacs of 1913, these new, streamlined Kops played straight to star comic Billy Bevan in such polished two-reelers as *Be Reasonable* (1921), *Nip and Tuck* (1923), and *Wandering Willies* (1926).

When the United States joined the war effort in Europe on April 6, 1917, Eddie voluntarily joined the Army. Returning to Hollywood once the war ended a year and a half later, he worked as an assistant director to Rex Ingram at Metro Goldwyn (Mayer would join the party in 1924). He later promoted his own system for learning the Spanish language; he was a radio disc jockey; and he played small parts ("never as an extra," he insisted) in movies and on television. But none of these occupations could compete with his two years at Keystone. Eddie kept in touch with Mack Sennett, visiting him when he was an eighty-year-old patient at the Motion Picture Home in Woodland Hills. On November 5, 1960, Sennett suffered a heart attack and died. Following a Catholic Mass, he was buried in Culver City's Holy Cross Cemetery. Serving as his pallbearers were original Kops, including Eddie. Later, when it was discovered that no one had thought to put up a headstone for The Old Man, Billy Bletcher rounded up the boys and paid for one. It reads:

Mack Sennett
1880 † 1960
Beloved King of Comedy

The King was dead, but his court jesters were enjoying a renaissance. This can be attributed to the highly entertaining compilation features of independent producer Robert Youngson. The first two releases, *The Golden Age of Comedy* (1957) and *When Comedy Was King* (1960), had audiences in North America and Europe howling at the same sight gags that had made their forebears laugh. It was at this time that Eddie became curious about the legal status of the Keystone Kops name. Upon closer inspection, he learned that Sennett had made no provisions in his will for the ownership of his most famous contribution to film comedy. For a fee of a hundred dollars—or two hundred; he didn't keep track—Eddie was able to secure the worldwide rights to the name (spelled with a "K" instead of a "C," to differentiate it from the Keystone Cops, a charitable organization associated with the Shriners). Both spellings, incidentally, can be found as early as July 1914 in *Moving Picture World*. The whimsical "K" version became more or less standard in the fifties, as in the title of the 1955 Universal-International feature *Bud Abbott and Lou Costello Meet the Keystone Kops*.

When someone legally challenged Eddie's claim of ownership, he turned to some high-profile Keystone stalwarts for assistance. Chester Conklin could vouch for Eddie's authenticity, having starred in a Keystone comedy called *Dodging His Doom* (1917), in which Eddie played the part of a "jail bird"; Conklin also recalled that Eddie sometimes played a Kop. Roscoe Arbuckle's first wife, Minta Durfee, also had memories of Eddie in that capacity. Erle C. Kenton, a writer and director for Keystone who later directed several Universal horror films, stated that Eddie played a waiter in one of the comedies he co-directed with Bob Kerr in 1916. Another future director, A. Edward Sutherland, also called to mind Eddie LeVeque during his time at Keystone. The affidavits provided by these industry veterans did not convince everyone of Eddie's authenticity, but they should have.

Determined to make the most of his stewardship, Eddie contacted as many surviving Sennett players as possible. It didn't really matter to him (or to anyone else) if those actors had appeared in uniform onscreen or not; the Sennett pedigree was enough for them to qualify for membership. The retirees willing to trade their golf clubs for a billy club included Chester Conklin, Tom Kennedy, Eddie Gribbon, Pinto Colvig, Charles Diltz, and Billy Bletcher. These men were then in their sixties and seventies, and they certainly looked their age. But putting on those familiar uniforms once again seemed to bring out their age-defying energy. The first major appearance of the newly reunited team was for a television commercial commemorating the fortieth anniversary of Gibraltar Savings and Loan in Los Angeles, on January 19, 1962. The cameras rolled and the Kops were back in business. Outtakes from this event make for fun viewing; you can sense the warm camaraderie in the group. (This footage can be found as a bonus extra of *The Mack Sennett Collection*,

The Keystone Kops trade in their 1916 Model T for a 1962 Volkswagen Beetle. Pictured are Billy Bletcher and Chester Conklin (up front); behind them are Clarence Hennecke and Glen Cavender; standing in back are Vance "Pinto" Colvig, Tom Kennedy, and Eddie Baker; seated in the driver's seat is Eddie LeVeque; standing next to Eddie Baker is writer John R. Grey; director Del Lord is at the back, wearing glasses. Courtesy of Randy Skretvedt.

Vol. I Blu-ray set from Flicker Alley.) Everyone is smiling, even (rather incongruously) the president of the financial institution, whom the Kops wrongly arrest and haul off to jail on the charge of embezzlement. The footage also includes a soundbite from Conklin. When asked the standard question about his opinion of the current crop of comedians, he says, chuckling proudly, "We used to get a lot more laughs than they do today!"

Another high-profile event took place at Buena Park's Movieland Wax Museum on May 3, 1964. Photos show the Kops enacting a silent movie comedy with the great Buster Keaton, then experiencing his own comeback. It almost seems as though the waxworks had come to life! Predictably, a pie fight breaks out and does not conclude until everyone involved is covered with pie filling. The Kops generated more publicity by crashing a birthday celebration for comedian Joe E. Brown. They also accepted invitations to appear in parades, at fairs, and at charitable events.

As the senior participants gradually retired (or expired), new members were enlisted to take their place: Noble "Kid" Chisell, Stan Lawson, Jay Colonna, and "Slim" Ray Barnes, although their connection to Sennett was distant at best. There were some novelties produced under Eddie's aegis, including a couple of 45 rpm records by a rock group known as Son's (*sic*) of the Keystone Kops. Unrealized projects include a newspaper comic strip, a series of Warner Bros. cartoons, and a musical stage play.

With the passing of Chester Conklin and Hank Mann within a month of each other in 1971, actual Kops had, to paraphrase "September Song," dwindled down to a precious few. From that point on, Eddie went solo, billing himself as "The Last of the Keystone Kops." For the sake of accuracy, he could have amended that to read "the last *performing* Keystone Kop," as there were at least two former members who would outlive him: Abe Goldstein and Hal Haig Priest. Abe had been an extra at Keystone, occasionally doubling some of the principal players. In later years, he became a circus clown named Korkey, whose comic persona (and ensemble) was that of a Kop. He died at the age of

Celebrating his seventy-second birthday, comedian Joe E. Brown (center) is named an honorary Keystone Kop at a party in 1964 in his honor at Port Hueneme. Helping with the cake are (from left) George Gray, Chester Conklin, Pinto Colvig, and Billy Bletcher. Eddie LeVeque sat out this event, but as Joe E. Brown would say, "Well, nobody's perfect." Courtesy of the Los Angeles Public Library Photo Collection.

ninety-four in February 1990, just a little over a year after Eddie left us. The longest-lived Keystone player was Hal Haig Priest, an American-Armenian athlete who won a bronze medal in diving at the 1920 Olympic games at Antwerp. When he died on April 19, 2001, he was 104. These men knew the importance of the Kops' place in history. In Eddie's words:

> The original Keystone Kops are as much a lovable historical curiosity today as Buffalo Bill was in the early 1900s. When I appear in public, people shake my hand. They have their kids photographed with me. They ask for autographs. Men pump my arm off. Women hug and kiss me. But they aren't hugging and kissing *me*—they are hugging and kissing *history*. The Kops still have that impact. Even Charlie Chaplin, when he came back here a few years ago [to receive an honorary Oscar], remembered the Kops with great, great affection. He had two bungalows at the Beverly Hills Hotel, and he was seeing very few people. But when I called his secretary and said I was a Keystone Kop, she said, "Come on down. I'm sure Mister Chaplin will see *you*. When I got to the hotel, there were dozens of reporters and photographers from all over the world trying to get to Chaplin. He wouldn't see any of them. But *I* was ushered in. I showed him stills of the old Keystone Kops, and tears welled in his eyes. He told me, "I'm sorry I never played in even one scene as a Keystone Kop. You boys were funnier than I ever was."[4]

At one point during our conversation, Eddie apologized for speaking so quietly: he explained that he did not wish to disturb his wife, who was taking a nap in the next room. The former Florence Gilbert, to whom he had been married since 1928, had been a professional artist, as well as an illustrator of the, at times, decorative title cards used in the silent era. It was obvious to me that he was very proud of his wife's talents; it also seemed apparent that she was not especially well. He told me that their

---

4 The comedian had apparently forgotten a one-reel comedy from 1914 called *The Thief Catcher*, which was considered lost until my friend Paul E. Gierucki discovered a 16mm print of it in a garage sale in Michigan. In the film, Charlie Chaplin is clearly playing a Keystone Kop.

fifty-second wedding anniversary was fast approaching, and that he loved Florence "very, very much."

I thanked this kind gentleman for his time and wished him, and Florence, a happy anniversary. It had been one of the most pleasant phone conversations I ever had.

Eddie would continue to make appearances in uniform until as late as 1986, when he was ninety. The death of his beloved Florence, and a broken hip, put an end to his performing days. The last two years were spent in a hospital. And then, on January 28, 1989, Eddie and Florence were reunited. They were survived by a son, two daughters, and six grandchildren, and were buried next to each other in Hollywood Forever Cemetery (section 8, lot 128). Under Eddie LeVeque's name, his marker proudly reads: KEYSTONE KOP.

Eddie and Florence LeVeque, out on the town in 1980. Courtesy of Michael Campino, who was a great help to the author in completing this essay.

SIX

Buster Keaton: Saluting The General

Courtesy of Jerry Murbach (doctormacro.com).

A trestle bridge has been set afire by a Confederate loyalist. A steadfast Union general believes that, despite the damage to the bridge, it is still passable by rail. He gives the command to the engineer of the *Texas* to proceed. The train makes its tentative crossing through the flames. Suddenly, the bridge collapses under the massive weight. The *Texas*—and the engineer—plunge into the river below.

This is not just a scene from history. It is a climactic moment from *The General*, Buster Keaton's legendary silent film set during the Civil War. It was produced in 1926, long before computer-generated effects. What you see on the screen is real.

In 2006, I was at an event commemorating the eightieth anniversary of *The General* in the town where it was shot, Cottage Grove, Oregon. Also present was eighty-six-year-old Mary Crenk, one of the last—if not *the* last—eyewitnesses to the filming of the *Texas*'s plunge into Culp Creek. She was eleven at the time.

"What was it like?" I asked her.

"It was loud," she answered.

Joseph Frank Keaton was born in Piqua, Kansas, on October 4, 1895. His parents, Myra and Joe, were touring with a tent show, presenting lectures, variety acts, and selling patent medicines. One day in baby Joseph's first year, he climbed out of the trunk that doubled as his bassinette and crawled, in Myra's words, "like a crawdad on a creek floor." Finding himself at the edge of a stairway, he fell headfirst, bouncing down the steps; he then stood up, a bit shaken but unhurt. Having witnessed this, the manager of the tent show, a former comedian named George A. Pardey, said to the boy's father, "Gee whiz! He's a regular buster!"

Joe Keaton liked the sound of that. Pardey, an Englishman, was using a typical English expression, meaning a resounding fall, the common phrase being "to come a buster." And the name stuck.[5]

Buster Keaton would soon join his parents' rough-and-tumble vaudeville act, now known as The Three Keatons. And what a strange act it must have been! The toddler was dropped, shaken, and thrown around the stage like a rag doll by his father. In time, this very young trouper learned that if he laughed at or even smiled at his own acrobatics, the audience would not. He therefore developed a deadpan (but still remarkably expressive) approach to comedy. This would ultimately be his trademark gimmick when he made motion pictures. Buster left the family act to do just that, becoming an onscreen sidekick to Roscoe Arbuckle in a series of slapstick two-reelers for producer Joseph M. Schenck, who happened to be Buster's brother-in-law. Beginning with his first film, *The Butcher Boy* (1917), Buster wore his trademark costume: a porkpie hat and slap shoes that were three sizes too big. No mere acrobat, he co-directed the shorts with Arbuckle. So impressed was Schenck with Keaton's innate abilities that he established a production company especially for him in 1920. The comedian was granted complete creative control over his projects. Keaton lived and breathed comedy, and literally risked his life to achieve the heart-stopping effects that were a staple of his films. Keaton's cameramen were always told to keep shooting until he yelled "CUT!"—or until he was killed. He made it out alive after each film, but he had his share of injuries, including a broken neck while making *Sherlock Jr.* in 1924.

From 1920 to 1927, Keaton and his imaginative crew turned out nineteen shorts and ten features. The most commercially successful of his features was *The Navigator* (1924), but *The General* (1926) is deservedly included on everyone's list of The Greatest Films of All Time. The idea for that Civil War epic was brought to Buster Keaton's attention in September of 1925. One of his gag writers, Clyde Bruckman, was doing some research on the Civil

---

5 In Buster's version, it was Harry Houdini who gave him his nickname. The Three Keatons shared many a bill with the famed magician.

War when he found a book called *Daring and Suffering: A History of the Great Railroad Adventure* by William Pittenger (Philadelphia, 1863). He described the factual account to Keaton, who agreed it would make an ideal film. After all, it dealt with one of his favorite objects: a train. "Railroads are a great prop," Buster told film historian Kevin Brownlow. "You can do some awful wild things with railroads."

The plot is rather straightforward.

> The year is 1861. Buster plays Johnnie Gray, a young Southerner who is unable to enlist in the Confederate Army because he is considered more valuable to the cause as a railroad engineer than as a soldier. His girlfriend, Annabelle (Marion Mack), and her proud Southern family unfairly label him a coward. The action starts when a group of Northern raiders steal Johnnie's beloved train, the *General*, unwittingly kidnapping Annabelle in the process. Johnnie races north into enemy territory to retrieve his stolen engine and his girlfriend—in that order. The entire film is essentially structured along the lines of a chase.

Joe Schenck apparently felt the project was worthwhile because he was willing to put up the $400,000 to produce it. By the time the film was completed, it would be over budget by nearly a half-million dollars. This excessive cost was due in part to the location shooting. Thirty-one-year-old Keaton was an avid student of history and was determined to make the film as accurate as humanly possible. "So accurate it hurts," was the way he expressed it. Since the action originally occurred in Marietta, Georgia, Keaton himself traveled there to scout out the locations. He was terribly disappointed with the area. Negotiations were under way with the current owners of the *General* to use that historic train in the film. But when the members of the Tennessee Railroad learned that their prized relic was to be the subject of a comedy, the deal fell through. Keaton's scouts had to set out to find the needed replacement train and railroad tracks,

Johnnie Gray (Buster Keaton) is castigated by his intended, Annabelle Lee (Marion Mack), for not doing the honorable thing, i.e. volunteering to fight for the Union when war was declared.

Johnnie Gray catches up with his train, the General, which had been stolen by Northern Raiders.

Johnnie daringly infiltrates the Northern army's headquarters, where he becomes privy to their latest strategy.

A triumphant Johnnie officially enlists in the Union army as a lieutenant. When asked his profession, he proudly states: "Soldier."

which brought them to the timber-and-mining town of Cottage Grove, Oregon. Keaton told a reporter that he had been through this part of the Willamette Valley many times when he was traveling with his family in vaudeville, but that he was usually asleep at the time.

On May 27, 1926, Keaton's crew rolled into the rural town with eighteen freight carloads of Civil War cannons, rebuilt passenger railroad cars, stagecoaches, covered wagons, houses built in sections, loads of camera equipment and a whole platoon of workers. Buster, along with his wife, Natalie (one of the famous Talmadge sisters), and their two sons, arrived in the family's big Stutz roadster. They stayed at the town's only lodging establishment, The Bartell, along with many other members of the company. Once ensconced in her room, Natalie maintained a low profile. She preferred working on needlepoint to socializing with the other wives and actresses.

Keaton took great pains to replicate the engravings from Pittenger's book, and eventually built the town of Marietta in the heart of Cottage Grove. The second floor of the town's biggest garage was leased as a costume and prop department. A commissary, run by professional chefs brought in from Los Angeles, was set up to provide meals for the staff. Crowds poured into the makeshift casting office, looking for jobs as extras. Even with most of the population vying for roles, there still weren't enough able-bodied youths to pose as soldiers in the mammoth battle scenes. Trainloads of Oregon National Guardsmen had to be brought in to compensate for this deficit.

Every morning at five o'clock the railroad line was closed so the tracks would be free for the filmmakers. To photograph the trains in action, Bell & Howell cameras were set up on a rebuilt automobile that was driven along graded roads next to the track. When parallel tracks were available, the cameras were secured to the top of a railroad flatcar. All day, every day, week after week, the *clack* of the movie trains could be heard moving up and down the line. Regular train service to Cottage Grove all but ceased.

One would imagine the townspeople would be upset by this inconvenience, but they showed the crew nothing but patience and understanding. This can be attributed at least in part to Buster's likeable personality. In contrast to his deadpan screen image, Buster was quick to laugh and smile. He organized several baseball games at Kelley Field and impressed the locals with his prowess as a shortstop. And during a community-wide picnic sponsored by the Lions service group in July, members of Buster's crew entertained everyone present with an impromptu vaudeville show. On a more pragmatic note, the residents appreciated the revenue that the movie company was generating. About fifteen hundred local people were on the Keaton payroll, and filming was going to go on for months. The townspeople were even able to forgive Buster for inadvertently starting a forest fire or two. The wood-burning locomotives had been equipped with safety devices, but they still emitted enough sparks to ignite the surrounding vegetation. One fire near Culp Creek was serious enough to do an estimated $50,000 worth of damage. Shooting was brought to a halt as a team of volunteer firefighters battled for hours to contain the blaze. Buster did his part by standing in his underwear and fighting the fire with his pants.

The summer of 1926 was an exceptionally hot one, and fires (not of Buster's doing) flared up in all parts of the county. Thick grey smoke hung over the area for weeks, making filming impossible. The crew finally packed up their equipment and returned to Hollywood on August 6. After filming some interiors at the studio, Buster and a small crew were back in Cottage Grove for two additional weeks. Finally, on September 18, the production wrapped. To celebrate the occasion, a drinking-and-fireworks party was held at the Bartell. Things got a bit out of hand as drunken revelers lobbed firecrackers down Main Street toward the church.

Buster returned to Hollywood—this time for good—and spent the following weeks readying the seven-reel feature for its New

Year's Eve opening. Never had he been so proud of a film. *The General* would remain for him the crowning achievement of his long career. Unfortunately, the critics did not agree. The New York *Herald-Tribune*, for example, called it "long and tedious—the least funny thing Buster Keaton has ever done." Apparently, the Civil War was still too recent for some audiences to accept as grist for satire. When the film went into wide release the following February, ticket sales were disappointing.

Buster was on the set of *Steamboat Bill Jr.* on Labor Day in 1927 when he was given some truly dreadful news. His days as an independent filmmaker were coming to an end. Joe Schenck had sold Buster's contract to Metro-Goldwyn-Mayer, where he would have to make films in accordance with that studio's rigid policies. That meant that the comedian and his crew could no longer think up gags while a film was being shot; they would have to submit a formal shooting script with the gags spelled out on the typewritten page. He would also have to take orders from Louis B. Mayer, and it was no secret that Mayer did not care for Buster's type of comedy, nor for Buster himself. Right after being told this disastrous change of plan, he was to film the scene where the façade of a house, during a typhoon, falls over him. He is spared only because of the judicious placement of a window frame on the second floor. Again, no trickery was involved. Buster stood expressionlessly on his mark while someone gave the cue to drop the two thousand-pound façade. The cameraman was so sure he would be filming Buster's death that he had to turn his eyes away to avoid the carnage. When the dust settled, there stood Buster, with nary a scratch. In his present state of mind, he said he wouldn't have cared if he had been killed.

Buster's trepidations about MGM were more than justified, particularly when talkies were introduced. He was handed scripts that did not fit his well-established character. He was forced to recite unfunny dialogue containing puns and lame jokes. As for physical comedy, there was very little, and anything that was deemed potentially dangerous had to employ the use of a double. Buster had a great line for this: "Stunt men don't get laughs." He tried to improve the films, saying there was nothing wrong with sound that a little silence couldn't fix, but the studio brass ignored him. It got to the point where Buster simply didn't care anymore. He was drinking morning, noon, and night. While filming scenes for *What—No Beer?* (1933), Buster's speech was so slurred and thick as to be unintelligible. He was given to fits of rage. His marriage to Natalie was over, and his two sons taken from him. In one drunken stupor, he married a woman he hardly knew. Finally, there came a day when it all proved to be just too much to bear. Buster suffered a nervous breakdown. He was carted off to a psychiatric clinic in a straitjacket.

The outlook was tough, but Buster was tougher. He kept working—not at MGM; Mayer had seen to that. No, he was relegated to Poverty Row, where he made cheap, derivative two-reelers for Educational and Columbia. Directors like Jules White talked down to him; he even had the temerity to tell the acrobatic Buster how to take a fall! Buster held on, however. He ended up back at MGM in 1937, not as a star but a $300-a-week gag writer. Because no one could perform physical comedy as well, he eventually found himself back in the big leagues, with a guest-starring role in *Hollywood Cavalcade* (1939), 20th Century-Fox's Valentine to Mack Sennett and the days of the Keystone Kops. The exposure was certainly a boon to Buster's career, even if it established him as a pie-throwing Keystone comic, not the brilliant, technically minded filmmaker he was. But a job's a job and he was grateful to Virginia Fox, one of his former leading ladies, for recommending his services to her husband, Darryl F. Zanuck, the head of 20th Century-Fox.

Buster's luck had clearly changed for the better. In 1940, he married twenty-one-year-old MGM dancer Eleanor Norris, his third wife. Eleanor was an ideal partner for the forty-five-year-old comedian. She was protective of him but did not stifle his need to perform his at-times dangerous routines. Eleanor even submitted to being used as a human prop in his live performances. Her memory of her husband's approach to comedy was that it was "very precise, very mathematical." In 1949, LIFE magazine published James Agee's hagiographical overview of the silent clowns, with Buster a standout. This led to his turning up in guest shots on the new medium of television. He loved it. Embracing his new "old-time" image, he made dozens of appearances on the tube, re-creating his classic sight gags and throwing pies. Except for The Three Stooges' Moe Howard, no one ever threw a pie with greater precision.

In 1957, Paramount Pictures announced the forthcoming release of *The Buster Keaton Story*. The screenplay, co-written by Robert Smith and novelist Sidney Sheldon, played fast and loose with the facts, even though Buster was credited as the biopic's technical advisor. Portraying the great comedian was Donald O'Connor, a multi-talented entertainer who had also been born into a vaudeville family. He idolized the filmmaker he was portraying, referring to him as "the D.W. Griffith of Comedy." Deb and I had the pleasure of meeting that affable actor/dancer in his dressing room following a stage performance in 1979. He shared a story about Buster that dealt, not too surprisingly, with a train, or in this instance, a miniature train. As O'Connor recalled, the first time he met Buster was at the Woodland Hills ranch house the comedian had purchased with the $50,000 he received for the screen rights to his life story. O'Connor found Buster in the garage, operating his electric train set, which was arranged on a table large enough to fill the entire room. O'Connor watched as Buster took a puff off his cigarette, placed it on one of the now-stopped cars, and watched the train carry the cigarette around the track. When it circled back to him, he took another puff. O'Connor had to know what on earth Buster was doing. He explained that this was his way of cutting back on smoking. O'Connor, Deb, and I laughed at the thought of this real-life sight gag.

Time has been good to Buster Keaton. Once considered Charlie Chaplin's inferior, he is now the reigning comedian of the silent era. Like Chaplin, Buster Keaton is a true genius, although I wouldn't have said that to his face. He hated the word, at least when it was applied to *him*. "You can't be a genius in slap shoes and a flat hat," he said crankily. My adoration of the man began in 1979, when I saw *The Navigator* at an organ store in San Marcos, California. What distinguished that occasion—in addition to the brilliance of the film—was that Gaylord Carter, the famed silent movie accompanist, was there, providing the rousing organ score. It was a small group (maybe thirty people), but the laughter generated made it seem much, much larger. I had always liked Buster's comedies (like every other junior film collector, I owned a Blackhawk 8mm print of *Cops*), but now my enthusiasm attained a whole new level. Such idolatry even influenced Deb and me to settle, for a time, in Cottage Grove, at least partly because Buster had made *The General* there. When I mentioned this to a local resident, I was looked at askance. Who cared about some old silent movie anyway? As it turns out, quite a few people.

In 1986, Kevin Brownlow and David Gill, of Photoplay Productions, Ltd., arrived in Cottage Grove with a camera crew. The visiting Brits were there to interview the survivors who had supported Buster in his efforts sixty years earlier. The footage they shot was used in their definitive three-part documentary, *Buster Keaton: A Hard Act to Follow* (1987). Another historian, John Bengtson, specializes in locating original sites used in Hollywood films of the twenties. His first book, *Silent Echoes: Discovering Early Hollywood through the Films of Buster Keaton* (Santa Monica Press, 2000), was a revelation to me. In the twelve years Deb and I lived in Cottage Grove (1984–1996), we must have passed one house hundreds of times, not realizing it can clearly be glimpsed in one of the film's closing scenes. Nor, for that matter, did I know that the barn adjacent to the Old Mill Farm Store (where I purchased bags of kitty litter) was visible in the background in a scene involving the recruiting office. Now, thanks to an increasing awareness of the film's historic significance, these sites are considered locally important landmarks.

In 2006, I was fortunate enough to meet Buster's granddaughter, Melissa Talmadge Cox. Melissa was seventeen when her grandfather died in 1966, so she had vivid memories of the man she knew as "Grandpa Buster." He was not demonstrative, which was fine with Melissa, who vividly recalls her grandfather reeking of cigarette smoke. He showed affection by teaching her his favorite game of bridge and letting her play with his electric train set. This occurred during her many visits to the Woodland Hills ranch that Buster shared with Eleanor, whom Melissa adored. There were Hollywood mementos on display in Buster's den, but Melissa was more interested in gathering eggs from the chicken coop located on the property. In truth, she hardly thought of her grandfather as a star. She was aware that he was frequently on television (on variety shows, in Alka-Seltzer, Simon Pure Beer, Milky Way, and other commercials, and on *Candid Camera*), but she does not recall seeing any of his silent films until long after his death. Two cherished heirlooms currently in Melissa's possession are the George Eastman Awards presented to Buster and his former sister-in-law, Norma Talmadge, one of the silent screen's leading tragediennes. Another heirloom, a rather morbid one, is the handgun that Buster loaned to Clyde Bruckman in 1955, unaware that the desperate comedy writer was planning to commit suicide with it.

Much has been written about Buster's troubled marriage to Norma's sister, Natalie, and the speculation regarding their relationship has been a bit harsh, Melissa feels. She loved her grandmother "Nat," and does not remember her as the deeply unhappy recluse of the Keaton biographies. It was, nevertheless, a bitter divorce that ended the Keaton-Talmadge union in 1932. Natalie, in fact, obtained full custody of their two sons, Jimmy and Bobby, and even changed the boys' sir name from Keaton to Talmadge. I gave Melissa a yet-to-be-published essay I had written on the Talmadge family, beginning with her great-grandmother, Peg Talmadge, the domineering stage mother of Norma, Constance (known to family members as "Dutch"), and Natalie. She passed them on to her father, Jim Talmadge. Apparently, what I wrote touched him deeply, as he cried when he read them.[6] He was kind enough to send me, by way of his grandson Brady Cox, a message of gratitude, which I received just moments before a public showing I hosted of the 1923 Keaton feature *Our Hospitality*. What is fascinating about that film is that it features virtually everyone in Buster's immediate family. Natalie is his leading lady, although care had to be taken to prevent her pregnancy from becoming obvious. Buster's father, Joe Keaton, has a small role in the film, during which he demonstrates the hitch-kick he used time and again on the vaudeville stage. And the baby featured in the film's prologue, billed as Buster Keaton Jr., would grow up to be the same Jim Talmadge.

While hosting the silent film lecture series in Eugene, Oregon, I took my regular attendees on a tour of the sites used in *The General*. My capable Deb was the designated bus driver and co-host of the event. Before the tour's conclusion, we had made most of the stops highlighted in *Silent Echoes*: the site of the railroad tracks (now paved over for a bicycle trail); the barn in the recruiting scene (which has since been destroyed by fire); Kelley Field, the spot Buster and his crew used for their baseball games between gagwriting sessions; and the site of Marietta's main street and Annabelle's house. This location reminded me of an interview I conducted in 1974 with seventy-three-year-old Marion Mack, the actress who portrayed Annabelle. A former Sennett Bathing Beauty, Marion possessed something rare for a 1920s actress: long, luxuriant hair. Buster was looking for an old-fashioned beauty to play his fiancée in the Civil War-era film, and Norma Talmadge's hairdresser recommended Marion for the part. Ironically, she had only recently bobbed her hair, but a wig solved that problem. Keaton personally hired the twenty-three-

---

6 That essay is included in the author's *Silent Lives: 100 Biographies of the Silent Film Era*, pp. 346-355.

year-old (with a curt "She'll do") at $250 a week. Marion liked the people she met while on location, although she found Buster to be aloof and unfriendly. She later discovered that he liked her when he began making her the butt of his practical jokes. One occurred during the filming of an actual scene, when the carefully groomed actress was doused with water. Something she said surprised me, that Buster was a heavy drinker, even at the time he was making what would be his all-time favorite film.

The highlight of the tour was the setting of the legendary train crash. Once we had gathered in this historic spot (normally inaccessible to the public since it is on private property), we were not anxious to leave it. For what a site it is, as scenic and unspoiled as it was in 1926! On the day of the shoot, three or four thousand local people had gathered on that hot summer day to witness what would be the single-most expensive shot of the silent era. Forty-two thousand dollars had been spent for the scene's exhaustive preparation—a fortune at the time. At three o'clock in

The climactic crash of the Texas, Culp Creek, Cottage Grove, OR, 1926. Courtesy of Jerry Murbach (doctormacro.com).

the afternoon of July 26, Keaton gave the signal to the six cameramen to begin cranking. The unmanned engine began to make its way across the tracks. The timbers of the bridge had been partly sawed, and when a dynamite charge went off, the bridge snapped in half, and—well, you know what happened next. The train's whistle was said to have emitted a long, mournful scream, signaling to the spectators that something catastrophic had occurred. A dummy had been left at the throttle to give the impression that a live engineer had perished in the crash. When the dummy's severed head floated by in the adjoining stream, more than one person in the crowd fainted.

The *Texas* would languish for fifteen years in the Row River. It was not disposed of until World War II, when it was sold for scrap. Now, all that remains of the shooting is a rusted old rail of the bridge, which juts out from the waist-deep water. Just looking at it filled me with a sense of awe—of Buster as an artist, of the timeless quality of film, of history itself. I could almost sense Buster's presence, standing next to me, remembering that summer day in 1926. And smiling.

SEVEN
Zoe Rae:
The Universal Baby

Courtesy of the Media History Digital Library.

During the 1910s, the name Zoe Rae was known to virtually anyone who went to the movies. But as the teens gave way to the twenties, and then the thirties, forties, fifties, and beyond, the public forgot about her. Even in her private life, that part of her past was never referred to. As a result, her co-workers, close friends—even her own children—had no idea that the mature woman they knew as Mom, Grandma, Missus Barlow, or just plain Zoe, had been a child star, adored by millions.

It was not until she was in the final months of her ninety-five years that she ended her self-imposed gag order. Retired videographer Gary Lacher arranged for Deb and me to conduct Zoe Rae's first, and last, interview in ninety years. And what a pleasure it was to spend a Monday afternoon with that delightfully unpretentious lady! She lived with her daughter and adult granddaughter on an alpaca farm in Newberg, Oregon. We showed up at Zoe's door, on time, carrying some Cecile Brunner roses that Deb had been lovingly tending on our patio.

She was born Zoë Rae Bech in Chicago, Illinois, on July 13, 1910. Her father, George, worked as a typesetter; her mother, also named Zoë, was a cashier for the Edgewater Beach Hotel. Despite being a two-income family, the Beches were of humble means. They occupied a one-bedroom apartment above a grocery store, which sat opposite a coal yard. Baby Zoë's radiant smile brought life to these dreary surroundings.

Missus Bech left her position at the hotel to spend all her time doting on her only child. As an infant, Zoë had the bone disease known as rickets. Her mother would spend hours each day exercising the little girl's legs so they would develop properly. Almost from the time Zoë was old enough to walk, Missus Bech was determined to capitalize on her daughter's winning personality by putting her into moving pictures. Conveniently located near their home was the Selig Polyscope Company.

"Remember," Missus Bech said as they entered a studio for the first time in March of 1914, "the director will tell you to do things and you do them! *Mama says so.*"

The director on Zoë's initial shoot instructed her to open a closet door and discover a dead body.

"React to it," he said.

Zoë gave it all she had. When the "corpse" fell out, she screamed bloody murder and collapsed in a faint. Everyone from the cameraman to the grips laughed uproariously at this amateurish display of histrionics. When the laughter subsided, the director placed Zoë on his knee.

"Honey," he said gently, "that was just fine, but that's the way a grown-up lady would react. Would you mind trying it again?"

She did. For the second take, her reaction was dramatic, yet believable. The director nodded his approval.

"Cut! Print!" he yelled.

By 1915, Los Angeles was the place to be if you were in movies. The film industry was rapidly taking flight; jobs were to be had by writers, carpenters, electricians, stuntmen, cameramen—and actors. Hoping for advancement, Missus Bech convinced her husband to stay in Chicago and continue to earn a living while she and Zoë chased after fame and fortune. They rented a room with kitchen facilities and a private bath in a boarding house on Pico Avenue. This was near the west coast branch of the American Biograph Company, for whom Zoë was to make at least a dozen short pictures. Biograph's best days were behind them since D.W. Griffith's recent departure, and the studio would soon close its doors forever.

Fortunately, Missus Bech received an offer from the newly opened Universal Studios, a motion picture empire located on 230 acres in the San Fernando Valley. In 1916, Zoë was signed to a five-year contract for the then-fabulous sum of $100 per week. Substituting her middle name for her last and dropping the umlaut from Zoë, the rising child star would be known as Zoe Rae by her ninth Universal picture, *Bettina Loved a Soldier* (1916). Her nickname was "Little Zoe, the Universal Baby." While the infantile moniker might sound a bit antiquated today, "Baby" stars were a mainstay in silent films, early talkies, and on the vaudeville stage. In addition to Baby Zoe, there was Baby Marie Osborne, Baby Peggy Montgomery, Baby LeRoy, and Baby Rose Marie. There were also the WAMPAS Baby Stars, a promotional campaign of the Western Association of Motion Picture Advertisers, which annually honored a baker's dozen of ingénues said to be on the verge of stardom. The campaign ran from 1922 through 1934, except for the years 1930 and 1933. Some of the future stars included Clara Bow, Fay Wray, Mary Astor, Joan Crawford, Janet Gaynor, and Dolores Costello.

Much ballyhoo surrounded the studio's latest acquisition, at least in the trade papers. One item states that the five-year-old was already a screen veteran with a hundred photoplays to her credit. So enamored of acting was Miss Rae, the article continues, that she even performed in her off hours, putting on skits with the help of her parents, her servants—even her pets.

"*That,*" Zoe said of the ninety-year-old publicity release, "is a lot of *crap!*"

The fact of the matter was that, while playing "dress-up" before the cameras may have been fun at times, it was also hard work, particularly for one so young. There were many long hours spent beneath the harsh glare of the blazing Klieg lights. Makeup presented a challenge at times as well. In *A Kentucky Cinderella*, a 1917 drama set in the pre-Civil War South, Zoe was required to "black-up" in the minstrel show tradition. To achieve this, a bright-red powder was dissolved in warm water and applied to her face, arms, and legs. (On the orthochromatic film stock, red photographs as black.) Add to this an uncomfortably itchy wig and a tattered dress and Little Zoe was one unhappy girl during the making of the five-reel picture.

"It took my father an hour at night to wash that awful red stuff off me," she told us. "Then it took my mother another hour to get the red out of the tub."

Despite these rather sour memories, *A Kentucky Cinderella* remained one of Zoe's personal favorite vehicles. The film survives in a partial print at the EYE Institute in the Netherlands.

Universal was famous for its westerns and Zoe eventually found herself dressed in the garb of the Old West. This was for her supporting role in *The Ace of the Saddle* (1919), directed by the legendary John Ford. Containing scenes shot along the Rio Grande, this Harry Carey oater featured an appearance by King Fisher Jones, the real-life cowboy who led American cattlemen against sheepherders in the Johnson County War. But then, there were plenty of cowboys, both real and make-believe, on the Universal lot during the teens. It was a rustic time in the studio's history. There was even a chicken ranch on the lot, which housed the white leghorns so prized by the studio's president and founder, Carl Laemmle. When asked how to pronounce his name, the German immigrant's stock answer was: "The name means *little lamb* and is pronounced as if it were spelled *lem-lee*." Affectionately known as Uncle Carl, Laemmle was notorious for his flagrant nepotism. Whether they were qualified or not, he appointed numerous relatives, including his son Julius, his nephews, and all of his brothers-in-law, to executive positions. The whimsical poet Ogden Nash is famously responsible for the couplet "Uncle Carl Laemmle/Has a very large faemmle." Zoe remembered the mogul not as the kindly "Uncle Carl" of show business legend, but as a cold businessman who was determined to get as much as possible out of every employee.

She had much fonder memories of one contract player who was then working his way up the ranks: Lon Chaney. Born Leonidas Frank Chaney in Colorado Springs on April 1, 1883, Lon was entertaining his deaf-mute parents from an early age with his God-given gift for pantomime. While still in his teens, he appeared in stage productions, often in comedic roles. As an aspiring extra at Universal City beginning in 1915, he had to compete with hundreds of others to earn a place on a working set. The makeup skills he had learned in the theatre gave him a unique advantage. He caught the eye of every casting director by transforming himself into a wide variety of characters. From his trusty makeup case emerged all manner of cheeks, noses, and ears—small wonder that he later earned the title "Man of a Thousand Faces." As a result, he appeared in 110 one- and two-reelers, only occasionally with billing. Zoe had a front-row seat for Chaney's unique artistry. He would call her over when they were each between takes and show her his latest creation.

"I was just fascinated by him," Zoe said with a smile. "He was a very pleasant gentleman in my eyes, and very dedicated."

Lon Chaney co-starred with Zoe in *The Kaiser, Beast of Berlin*, a propaganda film made at the height of World War I in 1918. Universal's PR department trumpeted the film's merits: "A sensational exposé of the private life of the Kaiser. It's the photo-dramatic sensation of all time—thrilling beyond words!" Whether or not this seven-reeler warranted such hyperbole is a matter of speculation: no print is known to exist. That it was an important film is apparent since it remains on the American Film Institute's Top Ten Most-Wanted List.

The Kaiser, Beast of Berlin is also noteworthy for the contributions of its director and star, New Zealand born Rupert Julian. A tall man with a military bearing and a stiffly waxed moustache, he bore an uncanny resemblance to Kaiser Wilhelm. Essaying the role of the Kaiser in three films apparently had a profound effect on Julian, as he was to grow increasingly imperious with his actors and technicians. Cameraman Charles Van Enger once described Julian as "screwy as hell," and routinely ignored his instructions. Lon Chaney also chafed at the director's dictatorial approach during the making of The Phantom of the Opera (1925). Julian appears to have been more successful with the distaff side. Actress Ruth Clifford, who co-starred with Zoe in A Kentucky Cinderella, considered the director kind and empathetic. Zoe, too, had nothing but praise for the man she described as a father figure. His wife, Elsie Jane Wilson, was a director as well. It has been said that she assisted her husband in directing some of his films.

In 1924, a fire in the Universal vault destroyed most of the studio's negatives. To free up more storage space, it was decided in 1947 that all the silent positive prints be intentionally destroyed. It is therefore a cause for celebration when one of those long-lost films is rediscovered, particularly if the print is in good-to-excellent condition. That was the case when my friend Michael Aus, of Rare Silent Films, learned of a complete 35mm nitrate print of a 1917 five-reel feature called *The Little Pirate*. Based on a short story by Norris Shannon and a scenario by Elliot J. Clawson, it was produced by Universal's Butterfly Pictures unit, directed by Elsie Jane Wilson, and stars Zoe Rae. The print had French and Danish intertitles, which Michael converted to English. Dozens of cineastes donated funds in a start-up campaign to allow for the obscure film's restoration. The following is my description of the narrative, based on multiple viewings.

> Businessman John Baird (Frank Brownlee) desperately needs cash to invest in a make-or-break investment. His financial advisor (a crotchety fellow, portrayed effectively by an uncredited actor) suggests that his client liquidate $90,000 worth of bonds at his bank. John goes to his wife, Virginia (the fine German actress Gretchen Lederer), to seek permission to use the securities. She gently reminds her husband that the bonds are not theirs but their adored only child's, Margery (Zoe Rae), a six-year-old given to wearing a bell-like ruffled dress and a huge white bow in her hair. John's financial advisor tells him that this is no time for scruples. Overhearing the discussion, his wife promptly goes to the bank, withdraws the securities, and pays a visit to the opulent home of her handsome young friend George Drake (Charles West). She asks if she may leave the securities with him for safekeeping. He consents, after which he offers to take her for a ride in his brand-new luxury automobile. While on the road, the car

malfunctions, requiring repairs. As a mechanic sees to it, George and Virginia share a meal together.

Following a leisurely afternoon, she returns home to John, feeling much more carefree than she had earlier. She tells him that she has reconsidered, and that he may indeed use Margery's securities as collateral for the loan. Suspecting that his wife and George Drake are having an affair, he coldly responds that he will go to the bank on the morrow to collect them. Virginia informs him that they are now in George's possession. John responds with undisguised contempt at this development. It all proves too much for Virginia. She tells him that she is leaving and will not return until he asks for her forgiveness.

John tells Margery that her mother has gone and will likely not be coming back. Instead of grieving, Margery optimistically concocts a scheme. She forges a letter from her father to her mother, admonishing his own egregious behavior and pleading with her to come home. She then evades a lovingly protective maid (Lillian Peacock) and heads straight for the stables. Mounting her pony, she says, "My little cutie, take me to the post office." The pony sets off as though he knows the way. While en route, Margery is distracted by the sight of a rabbit in a field. She dismounts and chases the woodland creature, possibly with the intention of turning it into a pet—or rabbit stew. Meanwhile, the pony wanders off, and eventually returns home, *sans* Margery.

John goes to George Drake's home and demands that he hand over the instruments at once. An alienated George goes to his office to get them, only to discover they are missing. He returns to John and states that the bonds have been stolen. With smoldering rage, John accuses Drake of having pilfered them. The accused makes it known to his adversary that, had he not such respect for Virginia, he would surely lay hands upon him.

Meanwhile, the little girl wanders aimlessly in the countryside until she is approached by a pirate—actually, a boy a few years her senior (Burwell Hamrick)—dressed in pirate garb and brandishing a toy musket. When he introduces himself as Captain Kidd, Margery responds, "Oh, I *love* pirates!" Swearing her allegiance, she agrees to join his band, of which she is the sole member. They board a rowboat, christened *The Jolly Rodger*, and six-year-old Margery is assigned to do the rowing, a rugged task at which she is surprisingly adept. Upon reaching the shore of an island, she follows Captain Kidd to his grass hut. Perched within is the requisite parrot, every pirate's best friend, and a frosted layer cake. Not bothering with utensils, the boy and girl each gorge on a large piece. Later, whilst lurking in some bushes, they espy a suspicious-looking man, who has come to the desolate area to bury Margery's securities. The moment he sets sale in his boat, the junior pirates dig up the "buried treasure." Uncovering them by hand, the boy believes they are valueless, but Margery hides the papers in her dress.

The parents' concern over the missing instruments now takes a distant second place to the formation of a search party to find their daughter. Everyone, staff included, takes part in the desperate search for the beloved Margery. Their relationship issues temporarily forgotten, John and Virginia unite in dread. "The house feels so empty without Margery," Virginia says sadly. John blames himself for everything that has transpired. In a separate location, Captain Kidd's mother (unidentified) is every bit as distraught over her missing son. "If heaven would only bring back my child to me," she says mournfully, "I would never punish him again."

The missing boy is reading a scary pirate story as Margery cowers in overdone horror. Her kohl-rimmed eyes with their extended lashes only grow larger and her quaking more exaggerated when a stray dog's howling matches that of the wolf in the storybook. They tentatively leave the hideout to investigate. The dog is highly approachable and soon joins in on the fun. He is left alone, however, when they go out to forage, a mission that yields exactly nothing. Returning to their hut, they find the dog fast asleep after having devoured the remainder of the cake. Aware that their food supply has been compromised, the boy and girl instantly, and simultaneously, develop severe hunger pangs. The thrill of pirating has been supplanted by grim reality. "I want to go home!" Margery wails, and the boy clearly yearns for the comforts of home and hearth as well. They once again board *The Jolly Rodger*, only this time Captain Kidd gallantly does the rowing. A serious problem arises: the boat has a hole in it, causing water to accumulate in the interior. The kids are frantic! Thankfully, the dashing George Drake sees them from the shore, senses their predicament, and dives in the lake, making a rapid approach to the sinking vessel. In the nick of time, he saves them. Greeting them onshore are their relieved parents. Margery's jubilant mother and father joyously hug and kiss their daughter. Captain Kidd sits on his tearful mother's lap, looking rather smug. Just then, his mother turns him over on her knee and gives him a sound spanking (so much for her resolution). The staff members of both the Bairds' and Drake's residences are present, including one bad egg (Frederick J. Titus), otherwise known as George's butler. A rough-looking sort, he is identified by Margery as the man she saw burying the bonds. She then produces the disinterred document. The other men forcefully take hold of the miscreant. George's maid now feels safe enough to tell of the abuse doled out to her by the butler to ensure her silence. As the camera must have been about to run out of film, a telegram conveniently arrives, announcing that

George had wired the needed cash at just the right time, resulting in a major financial windfall for the Baird family. Amidst all this coincidentally timed good news, Margery precociously announces: "When I grow up, I'm going to marry a pirate."

Although *The Little Pirate* is by no means a classic, it seemed to be well liked upon its initial release. One Canadian paper, *The Daily Colonial*, rhapsodically described it as a "delightful comedy-drama featuring the most beautiful and talented child actress in films." An article in *Moving Picture World* extols two of Zoe's newly acquired skills.

> Little Zoe Rae is always learning something new. In this picture she appears for the first time in the role of an equestrienne. Zoe is furnished with a fascinating pie-bald pony of her own in the first part of the picture. "Picture stars should all be good horsewomen," says the Baby, who never contemplates any other career than that of the cinema. Besides becoming an efficient horsewoman, little Zoe had to learn to row in order that the plot might be carried through successfully.

Yet another reviewer described the scene in which Zoe's character faces imminent death at the bottom of the lake. "This is where Zoe does some of her most extraordinary emotional acting. Her terror is as realistic as that of Madame Sarah Bernhardt herself, whom Zoe long ago adopted as her model." As odd as that reads, it is not far from the truth. If one were to watch a YouTube clip from the 1912 four-reel European drama, *Les Amours de la Reine Élizabeth* (or *The Loves of Queen Elizabeth*, as it was released by Famous Players-Lasky in the United States), they would see the "Divine Sarah" chewing the scenery like mad in her film debut. That style of over-emoting, known as the Delsarte Method, was much in demand at that time. Audiences, accustomed to attending live melodramas, felt they were getting their money's worth when actors on the stage or screen used exaggerated reactions and bold gestures. By contrast, actresses like Mary MacLaren were frequently criticized for "not doing anything" when giving subdued, ultra-realistic performances. In fairness, there are instances in *The Little Pirate* when Zoe's acting is credible. When she approaches her father for a kiss, for instance, she does not immediately sense just how depressed he is. At the moment of her realization, her body language and expression register concern and sorrow, and all with admirable subtlety. At other times, regrettably, Zoe had been coached to act with a capital "A." To express happiness, she does so in the cloying manner D.W. Griffith required of his ingénues: to jump up and down and clap her hands at the slightest provocation, and to react to nature's gifts with wonder, as in "Ooh … the little birds! … Ooh, look! A little bunny!" The results are, at best, unconvincing.

Another director Zoe recalled with favor was Madeline Brandeis. Born Madeline Frank in San Francisco in 1897, Brandeis is an interesting yet obscure figure among pioneering female directors. Her specialty involved making independent films geared for children. In 1918, she prevailed upon her wealthy husband to provide the necessary financing for her dream production of *The Star Prince*. The scenario of this imaginative film involves a little boy who believes he had been brought to earth by a falling star, thus elevating him to princely status. The five-reel fantasy was filmed under the banner of the Chicago Little Players' Company and features an all-child cast. Heading the cast is Zoe Rae, on loan from Universal. And in the gender-bending tradition of the silent era, she plays the role of the boy.

"They seemed to like me more as a boy than as a girl," Zoe said with a shrug.

Making this film was perhaps the most carefree experience of Zoe's career. She loved the woodsy setting, the animals, and her regal prince costume. She enjoyed the company of her equally youthful co-stars, especially the comically gifted Dorphia Brown, who plays the princess. Most of all, she adored her director, and the feeling was mutual.

When Madeline Brandeis divorced her husband in 1921, she claimed to be "the first woman in history to receive a million dollars in alimony." She would invest a good portion of that money in her own productions, none of which have survived the passage of time. It is particularly fortuitous that a copy of *The Star Prince* is available for reappraisal. A charming little film, it offers a vivacious performance by Zoe and an innovative use of stop-motion photography in scenes involving forest animals.

In 1937, Madeline Brandeis was the victim of an automobile accident in Gallup, New Mexico. Two weeks later she died of her injuries. She was thirty-nine years old.

Zoe Rae's filmography would come to include more than fifty documented titles, ranging from stark melodramas to breezy comedies, from one-reelers to feature-length productions. Her performances in these films inspired adulation from moviegoers around the world. A testament to that popularity can be found in the following excerpts from her carefully preserved fan mail:

- "Dear Zoe," begins a letter postmarked Lancashire, England, "Will you send me a photograph as you are lovely, such a dear little girl."
- "Please excuse me, an utter stranger writing to you," another admirer tentatively begins, "I am taking this liberty because your name is famous and much talked about among our students here in Tokyo."
- "I am sorry to be here in Denmark," laments a seventeen-year-old writer, "there are no girls as pretty as you in my country."
- And this touching missive: "Dear Baby: When I saw you representing sympathy, I was anxious to write to you. Will you be a correspondent with me? I live in Ponce, the second largest city in Puerto Rico."
- Finally, this unusual request from a citizen of Hoboken, New Jersey: "Please be a friend and answer this letter with a lock of your beautiful hair."

The year 1921 proved to be pivotal for Zoe. Her five-year contract with Universal was up for renewal and her mother was engaged in heated negotiations with Laemmle. These were brought to a sudden halt by, of all people, Zoe's father. George Bech declared that his ten-year-old daughter could not continue with her movie career until she had the benefit of a proper education. Zoe could not recall feeling even the slightest bit of disappointment over this decision. From the beginning, her parents had made it clear to her that she was nothing special—just an ordinary person. To reinforce this, she had not been allowed to watch herself on the silver screen, nor was she shown the fan magazine articles that referred to her glowingly as "the greatest little emotional actress on record." This strict upbringing apparently worked. Zoe blended in well with the other boys and girls in public school and earned good grades from her teachers.

By the time she finished college in 1932, she had matured into a beautiful young woman. Missus Bech once again sensed an opportunity and arranged for a photo sitting at the Witzel Studio in downtown Los Angeles. On the back of Zoe's 8 x 10 are the following stats: Height, 5 ft. 3· inches; Weight, 120 pounds; Age, 22; Eyes, blue; Hair, reddish brown; Singing voice, alto; Expert dancer." One can imagine the aspiring ingénue starring in the early talkie musicals then in vogue.

"I had always planned on returning to acting, so I didn't prepare for anything else," Zoe explained. "But the first time a casting director chased me around a desk, I was through. I said, 'I don't play that way.' I knew instinctively that was the only way I was going to get anyplace, so I told my mother, 'They can *have* their damned movies.'"

Zoe dabbled in screenwriting and singing before opening her own dance studio in Hollywood. This led to a fateful meeting with a fellow dance enthusiast by the name of Ronald Foster

Barlow. The two married in 1934 and would remain so until Ronald's death, sixty-five years later. They had two children, a boy and a girl, and knew the joys and heartaches of raising a family. Ronald was the breadwinner, plying his trade as a salesman; Zoe was a housewife, but hardly of the stay-at-home variety. Highly civic-minded, she served as the president of the Newport Beach school board. In their later years Zoe and Ronald moved to a Las Vegas retirement community, where they whiled away their days playing bridge, and their evenings dancing. It was, by all accounts, a good life. As stated earlier, the one thing Zoe did *not* do was wax nostalgic about her early days as a child star. This

Zoe, still smiling at ninety-five. Courtesy of Stephan Reckie.

changed in 2005 when a website dedicated to the silent screen mentioned that the one-time "Universal Baby" was still alive.

"Mom!" Zoe's astonished granddaughter called out, "Grandma's on the *Internet!*"

Perhaps because she was one of only a few survivors of the silent era, collectors began inundating her with email requests for signed photographs. Zoe failed to see what all the fuss was about. She never did consider herself much of an actress. When she was shown a video of *The Star Prince*, she laughingly summed up her performance in three words: "What a ham!"

Coda

Meeting Zoe Rae was an honor and a pleasure. As Deb and I were leaving, she said that she would send us a signed 8x10 portrait of herself as a child star. Just twelve days after our visit, Zoe's health began to decline rapidly. It was obvious to her daughter that the end was nigh. She gently told her mother that she had lived a long and fulfilling life, and that it was now time to let go. But Zoe could not. She had promised that "nice young couple who brought the Cecile Brunner roses" a signed picture, and she was not about to disappoint them. Her daughter selected an especially lovely one and handed it to Zoe, along with a pen. She inscribed the photo and handed it back to her daughter.

And at that very moment, she closed her eyes forever.

The inscription reads: "To Lon and Bambi (sic), Thank you so much, Zoe Rae, Universal, 06/05/06."

EIGHT

Kevin Brownlow: The Humble Historian

Courtesy of Marc Wanamaker, Bison Archives.

No one has done more for the restoration of silent films than Kevin Brownlow. His is the voice of the medium, a duty he first took on seventy years ago. "Silent films have always been a cause that needed defending," he explained. "The reason I was doing it was because nobody else was."

Robert Kevin Brownlow was born in Crowborough, East Sussex, England, on June 2, 1938. His parents, both professional artists, enrolled him in a military boarding school when he was ten. Although he detested the authoritarian environment, it was also where he saw his first silent films. The headmaster showed them on a 9.5mm projector every third Sunday evening, essentially turning the cafeteria into a cinema. Kevin was transfixed, particularly by the films of Charlie Chaplin, featuring Edna Purviance, who resembled his mother. Seated next to the projector, Kevin noticed that a few frames of film had been torn off the print and now lay on the floor. Discreetly retrieving the celluloid scraps, he could hardly wait to return to his room to further investigate this newly discovered form of white magic. Taking a flashlight and shining it directly on the film, he expected to see the image therein projected onto the white wall. It didn't work, but that hardly dampened his curiosity; if anything, it fueled it. Kevin now knew that he wanted—no, needed—a projector, and he begged his parents to buy him one. On Christmas morning in 1948, he unwrapped his very own . . . *slide* projector. Crestfallen, the boy realized he had not been specific enough; he had to have a *movie* projector. By the following Christmas, he had one: the Pathé Baby, a hand-cranked toy projector, along with two 9.5mm films. He then haunted the local camera shops and rental libraries, looking for worthwhile additions to his growing collection.

The first film he purchased was a condensation of a 1916 feature called *American Aristocracy*, minus the opening titles. Showing it to his parents one evening, his mother, a movie fan herself, said of the film's protagonist, "Oh, I know who *that* is—it's Douglas Fairbanks!" A studious youth, Kevin wanted to learn more about that specific film and star. He made a trip to the public library, which had only one such volume, a French book entitled *History of the Film*. Opening the book to a randomly selected page, he saw a scene still from, of all things, *American Aristocracy*, along with a paragraph detailing why the film is significant. As he later said, that was the moment he became a film historian. Inspired by Doug's gravity-defying stunts after seeing *Don Q Son of Zorro* (1925), Kevin jumped down a small flight of concrete steps at Waterloo Station and promptly twisted his ankle.

Like the rarity of film books in 1954, actual film prints were in limited supply. The camera store Kevin frequented was down to a single title: *Napoléon Bonaparte and the French Revolution*. He immediately suspected it was a dry, educational film about the French patriot, long on narrative and short on action. Buying it anyway, he was stunned when he finally viewed the film. "It was, to me," Kevin said, "the first glimpse of what I thought the cinema should be, in which everything looked incredibly real, and yet the camera was doing astonishing things that I'd never seen before, or since."

What he had unwittingly purchased was a two-reel excerpt of Abel Gance's 1927 French epic *Napoléon*. After a private screening for his parents, Kevin's artistically minded mother said, "That is the best one you've got." But among her contemporaries, she was in the minority. Others of her generation insisted that silent pictures were a complete waste of time: flickering displays of ludicrously bad acting and inferior camerawork. Explained Kevin: "I couldn't understand it because I was already a film collector and I was struck by the freshness, the vitality, the innovation, and the exquisite photography of silent films."

The excitement of this discovery inspired him to seek out other footage from *Napoléon*. He even wrote a fan letter to Abel

Gance and received an answer. Kevin was ecstatic. He planned to meet with his idol, who resembled, in his words, "a medieval saint." Despite the gap in their ages, and neither being conversant in the other's language, the two became friends.

Twenty-nine-year-old Kevin Brownlow (right) is clearly spellbound by what his idol Abel Gance is saying in this moment from July 1967. Courtesy of the British Film Institute.

When he left school at seventeen, Kevin became a trainee in the Soho cutting rooms of World-Wide Pictures. In the business, he heard much talk of the Al Parker actors' agency, and connected it with the actor Albert Parker, the villain in *American Aristocracy*. As Kevin recalls, "I rang him up, and said: 'Does the name *Fairbanks* mean anything to you?' He said: 'Jesus Christ! *Doug*? I directed him!' And I said: 'What did you direct?' And he said: '*The Black Pirate!*' I said: 'I think I've got one of your very early films.' He said: 'Bring it over.' So I took my little hand-cranked projector, and I showed it to him on the wall—and he was absolutely fascinated!"

Another pivotal encounter started with a dream, one that Kevin remembers from a director's perspective.

> I was dozing one Sunday morning and I imagined that I had at last gone to Hollywood, and I was being shown around the Motion Picture Home by D.W. Griffith himself. And he said, 'Over there is a room with a great cameraman. Over there lives a very fine editor.' And at the end of the corridor the telephone rang. And in my head I started tracking forward, as one does, and I dissolved through, and my telephone was ringing. So I went out into the hall and picked it up and a voice said, "Kevin, you'll never guess who this is—it's Harold Lloyd!"

Kevin at first thought this must be someone he knew playing a joke on him, but it was in fact the famous comedian Harold Lloyd. Sometime earlier, Kevin had sent the retired filmmaker a fan letter; Lloyd responded by inviting his perceptive young admirer to lunch at the Dorchester Hotel. "It was the beginning of a very fruitful friendship," Kevin said. "I loved him!"

In addition to studying films from an earlier era, Kevin had the desire to make his own. His first effort, *The Capture*, was based on a story by Guy de Maupassant. It has not survived. This paved the way for a much more ambitious project, made in collaboration with his partner, Andrew Mollo. *It Happened Here* is a dystopian black-and-white feature film depicting what life in Britain would be like had Germany won the Second World War. Despite its dark theme and somber tone, the film was well received. But the distributing company, United Artists, claimed that profits were not substantial enough to include remuneration for the fledgling filmmakers. Kevin was undeterred. "To me, film is a religion," he once stated. "I don't expect to get paid to make it, but I do expect total dedication."

Kevin was twenty-six when *It Happened Here* was released in 1964. It was also the year he went to the U.S., specifically Los Angeles, for the first time. While there, he managed to conduct twenty-eight interviews in ten days. Buster Keaton invited him to his ranch in Woodland Hills and even treated him to an impression of one of the ranch's chickens waiting to be fed. His new friend Harold Lloyd greeted him at the front door of Green Acres, saying, "It's only forty-two rooms, but it's home!" Unfortunately, he was stood up by the once-reigning queen of Hollywood, Mary Pickford, but they were able to meet at a later date. So impressed was she with the young man and his knowledge of her career that she said she wished he were her son.

Kevin hardly limited his list of interview subjects to actors. Some of the directors he spoke with were Josef Von Sternberg, John Ford, King Vidor, Henry Hathaway, Howard Hawks, Frank Capra, Fritz Lang, and—Greta Garbo's particular favorite—Clarence Brown. In 1966, Kevin, accompanied by Gloria Swanson, was given the rare privilege of watching seventy-seven-year-old Charlie Chaplin direct scenes for what would be his final film, *A Countess from Hong Kong* (1967), at London's Pinewood studio.

Kevin holds dear the memory of meeting the men and women who contributed so much to the silent era. As he said,

> They were the most extraordinary people I've ever met in my life! It was not just the stars and directors I interviewed, but the cameramen, the art directors, and even the title writers. I remember one of them, Monte Brice, told me that his first title writing job was literally taken off the golf course. Somebody had fallen ill; none of the title writers were getting anywhere near a good joke. And so he came in in his rather loud knickerbockers, and these tough ex-newspapermen all looked at him and said, "*That's* your title writing outfit, huh?" .... What he had to produce was a title which suggested that Al St. John had left for the city, had failed in everything he'd done, and was returning. He said to me, "God, send me a flash." I

said, "How 'bout this, boys? 'Al left home to set the world on fire but had to come back for more matches.'"

These interviews became the basis of his groundbreaking magnum opus *The Parade's Gone By ...*, published by Knopf in 1968. The origin of that title has always been interesting to me. Monte Brice was on the set for the misguided 1957 biopic *The Buster Keaton Story*. Brice could not help but notice that there were numerous anachronisms in the film. "They had it all wrong," he said. "I tried to tell them that things weren't like that in the twenties, but they wouldn't listen. I remember the assistant, a young guy. He said to me, 'Look, why don't you go away? Times have changed. You're an old man. The parade's gone by ...'"

Working in tandem with producer David Gill, Kevin made *Hollywood: A Celebration of the American Silent Film* (1980). The thirteen-part documentary series, featuring vintage film clips and newly shot interview footage of the era's last remaining participants, was commissioned by Thames Television. The series also benefitted greatly by the gorgeous orchestral score by Carl Davis, who would go on to win a Bafta and an Ivor Novello Award for other projects. The team of Brownlow, Gill, and Davis would also create individual documentaries on Chaplin, Keaton, Lloyd, Griffith, Chaney, Garbo, DeMille—all definitive, all exquisite.

Regardless of what project Kevin was working on, *Napoléon* was never far from his thoughts. While rewarding at times, the lifelong quest to reconstruct Gance's masterpiece has been fraught with peril. But Kevin Brownlow is not someone who gives up easily. His struggles with the project are vividly recounted in his published memoir *Napoléon: Abel Gance's Classic Film* (Knopf, 1983). Reading about the blood, sweat, and tears required to bring that lengthy epic back to life (while attempting to placate the mercurial Gance) is a stirring testament to Kevin's dedication to the art of film. In 1981, his first major restoration of *Napoléon* premiered at the Dorothy Chandler Pavilion in Los Angeles, with Carmine Coppola (brother of the director Francis

Ford Coppola) conducting the live orchestra. Deb and I were in the audience for that auspicious event. Particularly memorable was the triptych, the simultaneous projection of three reels of color silent film, creating a widescreen effect during a climactic moment. This concept was unprecedented when Gance utilized it in *Napoléon*'s initial release in 1927. The sequence was cut from the film after only a few showings and was not seen again until Kevin had restored it in the 1970s. As remarkable as that 1981 viewing experience was, an even more impressive presentation of the five-and-a-half-hour behemoth lay in the distant future. About which, more anon.

I had been aware of Kevin Brownlow since *The Parade's Gone By...* was first published. Naturally, I watched and enjoyed his documentaries, including the *Hollywood* series, during their original broadcasts. My enthusiasm for silent films, however, began to wane in the eighties when home video made film collecting obsolete. I simply could not get excited by tape. For one thing, it lacked the tangible aspects of film. The picture quality, too—particularly of older films in the public domain—was often exceedingly poor. It took the development of the digital video disk (DVD) to reignite my passion for silent film. Seeing the first few minutes of a Buster Keaton feature in a video store was a revelation—even the FBI Warning was a thing of beauty. Digital technology had advanced to the point where the film's picture quality of certain silent film transfers was undeniably striking, closer to its original nitrate glory, and light years removed from those dupey old prints I so cherished. More effort and money were put into these restorations, along with the synchronized scores.

Kevin admits to having been bitterly opposed to digital restoration until he was won over by a demonstration involving *Napoléon* in his London studio, Photoplay Productions, Ltd. In 1999, Kino Video released Photoplay's stunning transfer of Douglas Fairbanks's final silent feature (with sound sequences),

The Iron Mask (1929). I was mesmerized by the clarity of the image and the fullness of Carl Davis's powerful score. I was so impressed that I sent a letter of appreciation to Kevin, care of Photoplay. Knowing me, I probably laid it on a bit thick, but at least I was sincere. Within a week I received a reply from Kevin, in which he wrote that my letter had touched him. We have been corresponding ever since.

What especially impressed me about Kevin was his willingness to help writers with their film-related projects. I am but one of those who benefitted directly from his largesse. His files positively overflow with the transcripts of the many interviews he conducted over the years. There are also stills, letters, trade magazine and newspaper clippings—all of which he makes available to those who write to him for assistance. When Deb and I announced that we were planning to make a documentary film on our favorite subject, Francis X. Bushman, Kevin was among the first of our many contacts to offer assistance and encouragement. As he wrote in an email dated February 20, 2018, "I am glad to hear about the Bushman documentary, but I also feel a sense of gloom as I realise all the hassles you must endure to get it made." There were indeed hassles, lots of them, but Kevin significantly helped to lessen our burden. For instance, he arranged with Italy's Cineteca del Friuli that we obtain clips, at no cost, from Bushman's final silent, the long-lost epic *The Charge of the Gauchos* (1928). And when the staff of the British Film Institute were dragging their feet regarding some much-needed footage from Bushman's self-directed 1916 feature *In the Diplomatic Service*, I wrote to Kevin for help. As he valiantly replied, "I will be at the BFI soon and will take up the cudgels." His sterling reputation opened doors that would have otherwise remained closed to us.

When I was working on my book *Silent Lives: 100 Biographies of the Silent Film Era* (BearManor Media, 2008), Kevin read my manuscript and made annotations on a separate document, which he then mailed to me. At my request, he also provided the book with its insightful foreword. In it, he asks the question,

"What is the point of silent films?" His answer: "Silent films represent our history." Straight to the point, succinct—and so true. On a personal note, he also mentions his disappointment that, among my many subjects in *Silent Lives*, I had not included one of his personal favorites, Bessie Love. I learned much later that this fine American-British actress was the first silent star Kevin ever met. Appearing in a play at a theatre just a few streets away from his family home in 1954, Kevin noticed her name on the playbill for the local theatre and was flabbergasted. He sent a note to her asking, "Are you THE Bessie Love?" He told her he had a 9.5mm print of one of her films from 1916. He immediately received a reply, in which she expressed interest in seeing it. A date and time were arranged for Miss Love to visit the Brownlow home for the screening. As Kevin recalled of that momentous occasion, "We were all a bit concerned because the house we lived in had been very beaten up by the Blitz—bits kept falling off. My mother had put a very heavy curtain across the door to keep out the cold, and when Bessie came in, the whole pelmet fell on top of her. Luckily, we heard giggles coming from beneath and she thought it a huge joke. She turned out to be absolutely delightful and became a friend for the rest of her life. In fact, on the Hollywood series, we took her with us to Los Angeles to help us with difficult people—and she got us Mary Astor!" (Love was Astor's sister-in-law.)

The Oscar-winning director Martin Scorsese considers silent films to be sacrosanct. It was he who nominated seventy-two-year-old Kevin for a Lifetime Achievement Award. In his official letter to the Academy of Motion Picture Arts and Sciences, Scorsese stated that "Kevin Brownlow *is* film history." The board approved the nomination, making Kevin the first film historian and preservationist to receive an Oscar. On November 13, 2010, the Governors Awards were held at the Grand Ballroom at the Hollywood & Highland Center. Kevin, looking extremely dapper in his black tuxedo, began his speech by acknowledging those who had supported him in his life's work: Virginia Brownlow, his

Kevin Brownlow receives his much-deserved Oscar for film preservation at the Kodak Theatre in Hollywood, November 13, 2010. Courtesy of the Academy of Motion Picture Arts and Sciences.

wife of forty-one years; their daughter Julia; Andrew Mollo, who collaborated with him on two challenging films over a combined twelve-year period; the late David Gill, with whom he worked most prolifically on documentaries for twenty-three years; and for many years since with Patrick Stanbury. The niceties out of the way, Kevin then began to take the film industry to task:

> My god, your predecessors did a terrible job of preserving the silent era! Historian David Pierce is about to reveal that 73 percent [of all silent films] have been destroyed. That's like a publisher taking Tolstoy, Dickens, Scott Fitzgerald, and depulping every copy—and you can't even see the manuscript because they've burnt that as well. So it's up to us to do our damnedest to find the films that your predecessors destroyed and bring them back into the canon. An awful lot is being done, as you know—the recent find in New Zealand, the recent

generosity from Russia—but when I think of some of the titles that are gone, it's really heartbreaking….

I'll just tell you one terrible story which sums it all up …. Junior Laemmle oversaw the Collegians series at Universal. And there's a … swimming event, which one college wins, and they build bonfires and they come back to the college and have a wild party, setting the bonfires alight. But it doesn't burn, they don't burn strongly enough. And Junior Laemmle says, "Pile on the silent negatives; we'll never need *them* again."

And on that note, that cautionary tale, they burnt beautifully.

In March of 2012, Deb and I decided to splurge on something truly special: we would attend one of the public screenings of the third major restoration of *Napoléon* at the Paramount Theatre in Oakland, California, backed by a full orchestra conducted by Carl Davis. Given that we were about to be in the same place at the same time as Kevin, we knew this was our opportunity, at long last, to meet him in person. After checking for a time and place that was mutually advantageous, we made reservations for a breakfast buffet at the restaurant in the Waterfront Hotel, where Kevin and we would be staying.

On the day of the presentation for which we had tickets, we showed up early to the Waterfront restaurant. Deb and I weren't especially hungry; that feeling had been supplanted by the anticipation of meeting our esteemed dining companion. But when the appointed time came, we were still Kevin-less. I began to get worried that he might be ill. After fifteen minutes had passed, I called his room.

"Hello?" There was no mistaking that serious voice and that upper-crust British accent.

"Kevin?" I said. "Is everything all right?"

"Oh, yes, Lon. I'm running a bit behind this morning."

"That's fine," I said. "Just wanted to make sure you were okay. Take your time, please."

Before long, a lithe gentleman in a jacket and tie showed up, his hand outstretched, and apologizing profusely for being tardy. Despite his numerous accomplishments, he simply radiates humility. I conducted him to our table, where I introduced Deb. In our many communiques, he never fails to ask after her, nor does she ever forget to remind me to give him *her* best.

As the three of us were getting acquainted, a friendly-looking chap stopped by our table, grinning broadly. This was Kevin's cousin Timothy Brownlow. Naturally, we invited him to join us, and we are mighty glad we did. He turned out to be a marvelous conversationalist, a highly literate man with a convivial manner and a whimsical sense of humor. Timothy is an English scholar who taught at St. Columbia's College on the slopes above Rathfarnham, a southern suburb of Dublin, Ireland. Given that Timothy has literally known Kevin all his life, I couldn't help but ask what his cousin had been like as a boy.

"Oh, very serious," he said, smiling at the memory. "He was so curious about his study, and he pursued it with relentless dedication."

I had read somewhere that Kevin had been considered for the role of Oliver Twist in David Lean's screen adaptation of the Dickens novel. Apparently, Kevin's mother felt that her ten-year-old son would be ideal in the role. Having never seen a photo of Kevin as a child, I asked him if he was cute at that young age. He dolefully shook his head and stated, "I was half starved." What better qualification could he have to play a hungry orphan? Because Kevin went on to write the authorized biography of David Lean, I asked him if he happened to mention that long-ago aspiration to star in the director's 1948 film. He nodded and said, "I'm surprised I wasn't called for an audition. There's even a character in the story named Brownlow." It turns out that John Howard Davies, the boy who won the role, was a student at Kevin's school. Years later, the two even worked as editors for Thames Television.

The waitress came to our table and began to sell us on the all-you-can-eat buffet. Kevin seemed perplexed by this. "All I want is a breakfast," he said. "And some marmalade."

Now it was the waitress's turn to be perplexed. "What's marmalade?" she asked.

"It's an orange jam with rinds in it," Deb volunteered.

"*Rinds?*" I said with distaste.

Kevin shook his head and said that the world was in a sad state indeed when marmalade is not made available for breakfast. Timothy wholeheartedly agreed, saying, "Hear! Hear!"

Quickly recovering from the marmalade disappointment, Kevin authoritatively gave his order: "Coffee—*not yet!* Two eggs, sunny side up; toast, hash browns, and bacon, well done."

After the waitress left, Deb asked Kevin how the preparations for the show were going.

He looked unhappy. "Yesterday, we had the worst run-through in the history of run-throughs. At one point, the projectionist was testing the triptych—and one of the screens featured The Three Stooges!"

Deb and I laughed. We love the Stooges—doesn't everybody?

"I *hate* The Three Stooges," he said.

We laughed even harder at that. I then asked if he planned to introduce the film from the stage.

He shook his head. Like a silent film player, he doesn't speak unless he must.

"Well, how about if someone—*I'm* available, for instance—introduces *you* from the stage. I can see it now! The spotlight hits your seat as you stand and greet the throng …"

"That's SO American!" he said, rolling his eyes.

"Well, when in Rome," I said.

Changing the subject, Deb asked Kevin if he had seen *The Artist*, a pseudo silent film that won the Oscar for Best Picture of 2011. We had seen it in the theatre and felt very mixed about it. Apparently, Kevin did as well.

"The music was all wrong," he said.

"*That's* for sure," Deb said. "To think they would use part of the score from *Vertigo*! That's sacrilege."

"The other problem," Kevin added, "was the way the actors would silently make a speech, followed by an intertitle. As you know, the moment an actor's mouth starts to move, the intertitle is cut in, and it disappears the moment the actor stops talking. Other than that, I thought it was well done. I must admit, I felt a bit envious watching it."

I then asked him for his opinion on another film-about-film, one we enjoy without reservation: *Ed Wood*, Tim Burton's 1994 biopic of schlock master Edward D. Wood, Jr. (Johnny Depp). Martin Landau won the Best Supporting Actor Oscar for his dead-on portrayal of the aging *Dracula* star Bela Lugosi.

"Yes," Kevin said. "First rate." He then mentioned the music used in the film. "What instrument was that?" he queried. "I know it begins with a *z*."

"Zither?" I ventured. "Like in *The Third Man*?"

"No, that isn't it," said Deb.

"Yeah," I said. "It's something else."

"Yes," Kevin added. "But I'm certain it begins with a *z*."

This reminded me of the type of conversations I had with retired actors. When I could be asking about details concerning their careers, I was instead playing Trivial Pursuit. But then, that's how you really get to know someone. For instance, I asked Kevin about his health in general. He replied that he took a prescribed pill every day, but he didn't seem to know what it was for. And at one point, I asked him a question that seemed to annoy him slightly.

"So, Kevin, do you have any other interests besides film?"

"You sound like an interviewer for *Parade Magazine*," he said sardonically. "No. It's *film, film, film*."

I wish I'd had that kind of courage when my parents, or the occasional teacher, fretted over my obsession with old movies. Along that line of thought, Kevin opened his wallet and produced a newspaper clipping. It contained an academic's pretentious, indecipherable, mumbo-jumbo analysis of Herbert

Brenon's *Peter Pan* (1924), starring the gorgeous Betty Bronson. He proceeded to read it aloud, much to our shared amusement. Meanwhile, Timothy was having a marvelous time. He seemed to like Deb and me and the feeling was certainly mutual, so much so that he began to plan the day for the three of us while Kevin prepared for the showing. Timothy said we could "continue this leisurely breakfast," after which we could take a ride on a ferry, perhaps do some shopping, and after dinner, we would end up at his room at the Waterfront, where we could meet his wife Jenny and indulge in a cocktail or two. It sounded exceedingly pleasant, but I reminded him that we had tickets to see *Napoléon* that afternoon. Without coming right out and saying it, he seemed to think that *his* idea was scads more fun. Timothy is a party boy. Kevin, a confirmed teetotaler, is not.

The waitress dropped by to see how we were doing. "We'll take the check," I said.

Motioning toward Timothy, Kevin said, "Please put us on a separate tab."

"Actually, Kevin," I said, "Deb and I would like to treat you both today."

Kevin looked down in a shy manner. Timothy said affectionately, "Americans are so kind, so generous."

"Yeah," I said, "and kinda dumb."

A big laugh emanating from our table could probably be heard at the far end of the restaurant.

King Vidor, the eminent director of *The Big Parade* (1925) and *The Crowd* (1927), once said that a great music score supplies 50 percent of a silent film's emotional impact—just as a bad score can destroy the entire experience. Kevin told us about a showing of Sergei Eisenstein's *Battleship Potemkin* (1925), held in Trafalgar Square. A massive crowd showed up, primarily because of the group that had been hired to provide accompaniment: The Pet Shop Boys, described as an English synth-pop duo, who have sold 50 million records worldwide. About that experience, all Kevin had to say was "Oh, how we suffered!" On the opposite end of the spectrum is Carl Davis. His scores for *Safety Last!*

(1923), *The Thief of Bagdad* (1924), *Ben-Hur: A Tale of the Christ* (1925), *Flesh and the Devil* (1926), *The Student Prince in Old Heidelberg* (1927), *The Wind* (1928), and other films broadcast in the eighties on England's Channel 4, are as beautiful as they are evocative of their era. I was waxing eloquent on that subject when Kevin said, "I believe Carl is around here someplace. Would you like to meet him?"

"*Would I ever!*" I said. "By the way, what's he like?"

Kevin, who takes every question seriously, thought for a moment before coming up with three descriptive words: "Brilliant. Harassed. Temperamental."

"Has he ever gotten angry with you?" I asked.

"Oh, yes, *many* times," he answered. "But then, I can get rather belligerent myself."

"I can't imagine that!" Deb said.

"Remember Jack Oakie in *The Great Dictator*?" he asked, and then, with a self-deprecating smile, pointed purposefully at himself.

Kevin left, returning a few minutes later with the maestro himself. Carl Davis looked exactly like a conductor should. His grey hair was combed back and slightly overlong; he was wearing a dress shirt that was open at the neck, and he carried a messenger bag suspended by a shoulder strap. When he spoke, he uttered something about being English.

"Wait," I said, "aren't you from Brooklyn?" (I usually know a fellow New Yorker when I see one.)

He blanched slightly. "Why, yes," he said, his English accent slipping a bit.

"If I want to impress someone," I joked, "I just tell them that you and I are related."

"Yes, but *Davis* is just a made-up name," he said, apparently taking note of my Eastern European facial features. "There's gotta be a *vich* in there someplace."

"You're right!" I said. "My grandmother's maiden name was Nastanovich."

We had a good laugh.

"Seriously, Carl," I said, "your film scores are magnificent, incomparable. Of course, you're probably tired of hearing that."

"Well, thank you," he said. "And no, I *never* get tired of hearing that."

"Specifically, my favorites are the Chaplin Mutuals[7] and *Show People*."

"*Show People*," Kevin said. "We used a lot of that score in the *Hollywood* series."

Addressing both gentlemen, I said, "I only wish that *all* the films you collaborated on were available on DVD. Especially *Orphans of the Storm*, which I just saw on TCM."

Kevin said, "That's one score Carl *didn't* do."

Okay, *that* was embarrassing. Time to wrap this up. "It's been a pleasure meeting you, Carl," I said.

Kevin Brownlow introduces Carl Davis to Lon at The Waterfront Hotel restaurant, Oakland, California, March 2012. Photo by Debra L. Davis.

---

7 The Mutuals are a series of twelve superb two-reel comedies made by Charlie Chaplin between 1916 and 1917. Carl Davis has likened his scoring of these films to Wagner's *The Ring Cycle*.

"Same here," he said, shaking my hand with a smile and then making his exit.

Kevin looked suddenly uncomfortable. "I hate to leave you both," he said. "I have ... commitments."

"You're not really too fond of these events, are you?" I asked.

He slowly shook his head. "I never know what to say to people," he admitted.

"*Anything* you say is welcome," I said encouragingly. "After all, you're a rock star to this group."

"A *rock* star," he said with a smirk. "I'm trying to imagine what my daughter would say about *that*." Smiling at this thought, he left to meet his ... commitments.

Before Timothy sauntered away, he cordially said, "When the movie is over, ring me up. I'd love for you to meet Jenny. We'll have cocktails!"

That afternoon and evening marked the apotheosis of our silent film viewing experience. The restoration, and Carl Davis's score, were nothing short of spectacular. *Napoléon*, like *Intolerance*, with its sweeping story, quick cuts, and extreme length, is thrilling to behold. Thrilling *and* exhausting. By the time the triptych made its appearance, Deb and I were emotionally and physically drained. That, unfortunately, ruled out the possibility of a nightcap with Timothy and Jenny.

The following morning, we were seated at the same table in the same restaurant, probably eating the same thing we had the day before. Deb, who had a view of the entire place, said, "There's Kevin!" And sure enough, he was sitting all alone at a table, reading a newspaper. "We can tell him we remembered the type of musical instrument used in *Ed Wood*."

Absorbed by the newspaper, Kevin didn't see us coming. When we got his attention, he immediately stood up, a gentleman to the core.

Deb said one word: "Theremin."

"*Oh*, you mean *Zeremin*," he countered, grinning broadly.

Kevin and Lon.

NINE

Baby Peggy: The Last Silent Star

Diana Serra Cary and her famous alter-ego, Baby Peggy, Gustine, CA, 2007. Photo by Jeff Benziger.

Long before I saw a Baby Peggy film, I knew and admired Diana Serra Cary. Intelligent, beautifully spoken, and elegant are just some of the favorable adjectives that come to mind when I think of her. In the many years of our friendship, we spoke on the phone countless times, and the best of our conversations had less to do with her early movie career and more to do with the political scene, Catholicism and faith in general, people in the news that we liked or detested, societal trends, and the anomaly of human nature in all its permutations.

There was one topic, however, that I was reluctant to address, and that is my general dislike of child actors. Few things make my skin crawl like the sight or sound of Shirley Temple, that saccharine-sweet voice and just-too-cute manner. When I finally found the gumption to state this prejudice aloud, she laughed and said she couldn't agree more—and she had personally known Shirley Temple for most of her life! My assumption that Diana's youthful avatar, the silent screen's Baby Peggy, was like Miss Temple, only with the mute button mercifully on, could not have been more wrong. For her character of Baby Peggy was neither sickeningly sweet nor precocious. She was a pragmatist, attending to business in a no-nonsense, unaffected manner. And her acting, particularly in the features, had a depth to it that rivaled many older dramatic actors. This was confirmed for me when I sat down, alone, to watch a DVD of her 1924 silent feature *Captain January*. It was both entertaining and deeply moving. When *she* wept, *I* wept.

Jack Montgomery was a stuntman who doubled for western star Tom Mix. Jack's wife, Marion, was a pretty woman with aspirations to be in the movies, just like everyone else in the newly minted film capital of Hollywood. Jack knew what kind of bums hung around those places, and he wasn't about to let his shapely wife anywhere near one. He would have seen red if he knew that Marion had disobeyed him one morning by accompanying a neighbor woman on an errand to the Century barn on Sunset Boulevard, where they cranked out two-reel comedies featuring a chimp named Joe Martin.

Excited by her daring, Marion took along the couple's eighteen-month-old baby, Peggy Jean. Setting the child on a stool, she wagged an index finger at her and ordered her to "Stay put," while she and her neighbor completed the errand. The studio's leading director, Fred C. Fishback, saw the stoic child sitting so still she could have been a statue. In addition to her innate sense of obedience, Peggy Jean had that certain something a camera loves, and which makes moviegoers voluntarily part with their nickels to see. When Marion returned to pick up her child and leave, Fishback told her he wanted to hire the little girl at $150 a week. Of course, this meant that Marion would have to confess to Jack that she had gone against his express orders, but a quarrel would be worth it if Peggy Jean could bring in that kind of money. It took some fast talking on Marion's part, but Jack finally relented.

Baby Peggy (the studio dropped the *Jean* and added the *Baby*) was admonished by her father to follow her director's instructions to the letter. Her compliant manner did not allow her to trust her first co-star, Brownie the Wonder Dog, however. The little girl was afraid of the large canine, and in their first publicity photo together her uncertainty is palpable. The public responded favorably to the pairing in a two-reeler called *Playmates* (1921), so the two were stuck together, for a while at least. The short's success had prompted the studio heads to sign Peggy Montgomery to a long-term contract. And because she found favor with a four-footed co-star, she was paired with Teddy, a Great Dane who had achieved stardom in such Mack Sennett comedies as *Teddy at the Throttle* (1917). His current film, *Sea Shore Shapes* (1921), took place at Santa Monica beach, where the waves that day were running ten feet high. According to the scenario, Teddy was supposed to pick up Baby Peggy by the back of her one-piece wool bathing suit, trot out to the water, and hold her under for a few seconds before returning to the safety of the shore. The toddler had never been in water any deeper than a bathtub and she had never worked with Teddy. Holding her in his massive jaws, he dipped her in the water and seemed to lose track of time. Peggy tried to hold her breath, but water was rushing into her lungs at an alarming rate. She struggled, choked, and finally blacked out. When she came to, she heard Teddy's trainer telling him to drop her in front of the camera. He did, and the director yelled, "Cut! Print!" No one asked the half-drowned infant if she was okay. There was another scene to shoot and, besides, they were losing the light.

One gimmick of the Century Comedies involved Baby Peggy burlesquing then-current stars. Amid a desert setting and dressed in a burnoose, the little girl spoofs Rudolph Valentino in *The Sheik*. She also poses as operatic diva Geraldine Farrar as Carmen, as well as Wallace Reid in the guise of Carmen's fiery lover Don José. A questionable still (as seen on the title page of this essay) shows the innocent phenom as the sexually charged Pola Negri, smoking a cigarette. A more suitable genre was the traditional fairy tale. Moviegoers young and old alike enjoyed seeing Baby Peggy as Little Red Riding Hood, the distaff member of those breadcrumb-scattering siblings Hansel and Gretel, and Jack the giant killer. The giant, a nineteen-year-old Polish Jew named Jack Earle, hailed from El Paso, Texas. Plagued by a rare glandular condition and painfully shy, he wanted nothing more than to be invisible, but at a reported eight-foot-six that was not a likely option. To help raise Jack's morale, his father took him on a trip to Hollywood, which included a tour of the Century barn. Fred Fishback told the young man that he could earn some money by working in films. Jack gratefully accepted the offer, ultimately appearing in twenty-five Baby Peggy two-reelers, including *Jack and the Beanstalk* (1923).

In Jack and the Beanstalk *(1923), Baby Peggy plays opposite a real-life giant, Jack Earle, who at eight-foot-six was advertised as the world's tallest man. Following his tenure at Century, Earle joined the Barnum & Bailey Circus. He died in 1952 at the age of forty-six. Courtesy of the Media History Digital Library.*

Slapstick may have been the order of the day at Century, but Universal City was the place of westerns and melodramas. Universal's founder and president, the avuncular Carl Laemmle, had a saying: "A child star should make you cry." Charlie Chaplin was then in the production phase of his first full-length feature, which would mark the official debut of the adorable six-year-old Jackie Coogan. When *The Kid* was released in 1921, audiences around the world could be heard laughing and crying while watching Chaplin's charismatic find. It was this film that brought about the child star era, and Baby Peggy was to ride the crest of it with Jackie. Moviegoers who had stood in long lines to see her first feature, *The Darling of New York* (1923), directed by former star King Baggot, dampened their handkerchiefs as the crying little girl faced the prospect of a horrific death in a room that had been set ablaze. The fact that the situation and the child's terror were all too real would only have heightened the impact. Fortunately, she kept her head and managed to escape through an open window on the burning set.

The years 1923 and '24 marked the apex of Baby Peggy's film career. Independent producer Sol Lesser hired the cash-calf away from Universal to star in three features, *Captain January*, *Heidi*, and *Helen's Babies*. For this, Baby Peggy would receive the staggering sum of $1.5 million, plus a five-hundred-thousand-dollar bonus and a nationwide personal-appearance tour with each film. Peggy's father, now her manager, would be entitled to 50 percent of the box-office take from each theatre. Profits were to be split evenly between the two men. Meanwhile, Jack Montgomery's five-year-old daughter was feeling the weight of the world while starring in an expensively made drama about an old lighthouse keeper (the excellent Hobart Bosworth) and his conscientious assistant, Captain January (Baby Peggy). Peggy was instructed to cry at one point in the film. To make the tears flow, the musicians on set would play "My Buddy," a sad song that got to her every time.

Following the release of *Captain January*, Lesser placed a full-page ad in the trades bearing the headline, "The Biggest Little Star." He addresses potential exhibitors thusly:

> After reading reports on the Mark Strand Theatre, New York, the world premiere showing of Baby Peggy in "Captain January," I am free to express the belief that, in this big little star, Principal Pictures Corporation has a box-office attraction for consistent value to the exhibitor that is without an equal in the industry today.

The triumph of *Captain January* was followed by *Helen's Babies*, a domestic comedy in which our heroine co-stars with newcomers Edward Everett Horton and "It" Girl Clara Bow. A stunt which Jack allowed Baby Peggy to do involved her hanging from a tree limb until a convertible automobile (driven by Miss Bow) passes directly beneath her. At that precise moment, Jack gave the signal for his daughter to let go of the limb and drop into the open automobile's backseat.

Risking her life to entertain the public was not without its perks, at least for her father. Anticipating the cash that would no doubt pour in once the movies were released, Jack Montgomery ordered a custom-made fire-engine-red Duesenberg luxury automobile. He also purchased a horse ranch, as well as a Beverly Hills mansion, outfitted with a full staff of servants. (It should be mentioned that this was long before the implementation of The Coogan Law, inspired by the equally sad case of Jackie Coogan, to protect the industry's youthful actors from their own greedy parents.)

During a trip to New York, Jack took his famous daughter to see a show at the Winter Garden Theatre starring "The World's Greatest Entertainer," Al Jolson. Petty, arrogant, and insecure, Jolie took offense that the audience seemed momentarily more interested in the tiny silent star than in watching *him*. Stopping mid-song, he blurted out, "Yes, ladies and gentlemen, that's Baby Peggy in the box up there! Now, everybody take a good look at her and then pay attention to *me*! Remember, *I'm* the one you paid to see!"

It is difficult to convey just how famous Baby Peggy was at this high point in her career. She was the flag-waving mascot, standing alongside presidential nominee Franklin Delano Roosevelt, at the 1924 Democratic National Convention in Chicago. Crowds pressed their faces up against the windows of the restaurants at which she and her family were dining. She served as the prototype for children's dolls. She was mentioned in the same breath as Charlie Chaplin, Mary Pickford, and Douglas Fairbanks. She and her mother had even been Mary and Doug's special guests at Pickfair. In 1924 alone, a million fan letters addressed to Baby Peggy poured into the Universal Studios mailroom, completely overwhelming the six secretaries hired to answer them.

Just as the Baby Peggy fad soared, so too did it plummet. The reasons for her becoming persona non grata at age seven were:

1. She lost her front teeth, making her temporarily unphotogenic, and
2. Her hot-headed father had picked one fight too many with studio heads. He was then suing Sol Lesser, who had produced *Captain January* and *Helen's Babies*, two popular but, according to Lesser, unprofitable pictures. This, after boasting in print that his big little star was without an equal in terms of consistent value to the exhibitor.

Canceling their contract, Lesser never starred Baby Peggy in a screen version of the classic Swiss novel *Heidi*. Instead, she was over at Chadwick, one of Hollywood's notorious Poverty Row studios, starring in the low-budget *April Fool* (1926). Jack Montgomery had demonstrated a magician's ability in handling his famous daughter's fortune: he made it all disappear. But the magician still had some tricks up his sleeve. How about a big-time vaudeville tour? The ballyhoo would be terrific:

Baby Peggy in Person!
Six Big Acts!
Starts Wednesday!
Continuous Performance!

An act was hastily concocted. Appropriate for a movie star, it begins with a film clip, in which the one-time moppet is chased on foot by a policeman. When the curtain rises, a slightly taller, more mature-looking Baby Peggy is onstage, exchanging wisecracks with the policeman, now played by the inexperienced Jack Montgomery. The second part of the act allowed Peggy to work "in one," demonstrating her impersonation of Broadway and vaudeville titan Ethel Barrymore ("That's all there is, there isn't any more."). The finish had Baby Peggy performing a song-and-dance number à la Sir Harry Lauder, dressed in the Scotsman's trademark kilt and wearing a Tam o' Shanter. Booked on the prestigious Keith-Orpheum circuit, when she played that mecca of vaudeville, The Palace Theatre at 1564 Broadway, there were no congratulatory messages from her fellow performers. Their ungenerous position was that she had not earned her place on the bill, slowly but steadily working her way up the show business ladder as they had; she was merely an interloper from the movies. Still, she had to be in costume, ready to go out on the stage and please the customers multiple times a day. When she was brought low by the stomach flu, the show still had to go on, and she with it. A bucket was placed discreetly offstage for her convenience.

Talkies came along, rendering vaudeville redundant, and Peggy was delighted. She would rather live on the fifteen-hundred-acre Wyoming ranch her father bought with her hard-earned money. To help make ends meet, the Montgomerys began offering chicken dinners on Sundays. This was an efficiently run family operation and the results were delicious. Hungry diners enjoyed fried chicken (or chicken and dumplings), vegetables, mashed potatoes, biscuits, sage honey, an individual salad, a homemade dessert and coffee, and all for $1.50. No wonder folks from as far away as Cheyenne showed up regularly for these feasts. Of course, behind the scenes the work was arduous. Jack and Marion were the jovial hosts; their other daughter, Louise, waited four long tables seating a dozen diners each; and the ex-headliner was in the kitchen turning biscuits, whipping potatoes, shelling peas, and slicing pie. The diners began arriving at noon, and Peggy was still washing and drying dishes until long after sundown. The following day, she would be busy again, this time plucking chicken carcasses. As she whimsically described it, "It was 'continuous performance' all over again—only this time with feathers!"

Although basking in the great outdoors of Wyoming, the ten-year-old continued to be haunted by the specter of Baby Peggy. Once, while in town, she heard her "bow music," "Baby Face,"

being played over a loudspeaker. She dropped whatever she was doing and ran and didn't stop running for several blocks, so determined was she to escape her troubled past. She even symbolically buried Baby Peggy under a Douglas Fir high up on Jelm Mountain. As she sat by the imaginary grave, she felt at peace, possibly for the first time in her life. She also began to read voraciously; after all, she hoped to be a writer one day. Whenever the opportunity presented itself, she talked with the assorted Scandinavians in the area; or, more accurately, *they* talked, and *she* listened. This proved to be excellent training for her future as a biographer. Along with her autodidacticism, she began to attend school for the first time. She and her sister Louise rode their own horses four miles to and from the one-room schoolhouse every weekday. Peggy completed all eight grades in just three years. Her best subjects, not surprisingly, were history and English composition.

Following the Wall Street Crash, which occurred on Peggy's eleventh birthday, October 29, 1929, Jack informed his wife that a so-called business partner had robbed the family of what remained of their daughter's vaudeville earnings of $650,000; this was in addition to Jack's own bad investments and overspending. The devastating news only added to the tremendous strain existing between Jack and Marion, the latter accusing her husband of having "lost all of the baby's money." This so incensed Jack that he brandished a pistol, threatening to kill himself and the rest of the family.

With mortgage payments overdue, it was time to surrender the ranch and go back to Hollywood to see if there was another fortune awaiting the now-twelve-year-old has-been.

Hollywood had lost much of its glamour in the six years since Baby Peggy's last film, in 1926. All that was available to her now was "working extra," which her new agent (who had once represented Valentino) forbade her from accepting. Before long, the Montgomery family was stone broke and unable to pay rent or purchase food. Meanwhile, on the weekends, Peggy was volunteering her time and faded celebrity to assist at the teas for the Motion Picture Relief Fund. The one good thing that came from this venture was the food coupons she was quietly given to exchange for groceries at certain stores. It got to the point where each member of the family, the sole exception being Jack, was taking as many extra jobs as possible, working for $3.20 per day. Like every other town across the country, the Depression had cast a pall over Hollywood. Many silent film stars, made obsolete by talkies, were destitute after losing their fortunes in the stock market crash. Suicides of former movie favorites were so common that their notices were relegated to the back page of the local dailies.

In February 1934, Peggy and Louise were enrolled at the Lawlor School, with monthly tuition being twenty-five dollars for each girl. Jack viewed this as an opportunity for his daughters to be spotted by talent scouts. The student body during the Montgomery girls' tenure included Betty Grable, Jean Darling (of the silent Our Gang comedies), Jane Withers, Mickey Rooney, Frankie Darro, and Frances Ethel Gumm, better known as Judy Garland. Not surprisingly, Mickey would occasionally take over the class, emceeing impromptu shows featuring his talented classmates. The only thing their teacher could do was sit back and watch.

A much-needed windfall came to Jack when Sol Lesser called him out of the blue one day. Lesser said he knew Jack and his family were struggling financially. Perhaps a payment of six hundred dollars for his half of the rights to *Captain January*, and the unproduced *Heidi*, might help him out. Jack quickly accepted the offer. Only later did he realize that Lesser had pulled a fast one; he had purchased, for peanuts, the rights to what soon would be two blockbuster vehicles for Shirley Temple at Fox.

At sixteen, Peggy met Gordon Ayres, a fellow bit player, on the set of *Ah Wilderness!* The two were married in 1938 despite strong objections from Jack and Marion, who had no faith in Gordon's ability to provide for their youngest daughter. Their concern was valid. Peggy and Gordon were constantly broke and lived on borrowed money and charity baskets, leaving Peggy's self-esteem, in her words, "raw and bleeding." Always on the lookout for publicity—and more than willing to lie to get it—Gordon got his name in Walter Winchell's influential column with the following item:

> Two former child stars, now husband and wife, have been living in a small furnished room with only doughnuts to eat. They are Peggy Montgomery, once the famous Baby Peggy, and Gordon Ayres, one of the original members of Our Gang.... Surely the Hollywood casters will do something about these people????

Mortified beyond words, Peggy charged around the room like a caged bull. Unable to vent her anger toward others, she turned her rage on Baby Peggy. *She* started this nightmare, and *she* continued to be an unwelcome presence in her life. Having symbolically buried that kid years earlier, she was now willing to commit out and out murder.

A message arrived, stating that Maurice Kosloff, a former choreographer for Cecil B. DeMille's company, was interested in meeting with the former Baby Peggy about a job offer. The smooth-talking Russian told her in a face-to-face meeting that he would pay her $100 a week to audition children for the acting school he was adding to his ballet company. In addition to allowing her screen appellation to be used in all manner of advertising, the former star's job would be to tell the individual parents that their child could well be the next Baby Peggy, a second Shirley Temple, this generation's Jackie Coogan. The prospect of making $400 a month during the war years was difficult to turn down, but Peggy simply could not bring herself to mislead these hopefuls with what amounted to a scam. She rejected Kosloff's offer by saying, "I guess I'm just not hungry enough."

Immediately cold, he replied, "I can always get Jackie Coogan. I hear he's hungry too."

By this time, the name *Peggy* had become anathema to her. Ever the adapter, she began calling herself Diana, and she encouraged others to do the same. It was a step in the right direction. Meanwhile, Gordon was still pursuing his show business dreams. One day, Diana received a postcard from her husband, stating that the show he was touring in had closed in Provo, Utah. He signed off by saying he was Broadway bound. Diana realized she had been dumped. After not hearing another word from him for a year and a half, and facing near starvation, she applied for a job as a telephone operator in Monterey. She was immediately hired and managed to live well enough on the $28.50 she earned each week. When Gordon finally returned home, he made it clear that he would only be staying long enough to get a divorce. It seems he had met this terrific girl at an Arthur Murray studio, and they worked up a dance act in the Catskills. This, for Diana, was the final indignity. The one circuit big-time vaudevillians scorned as the lowest rung of show business was the Borsht Belt. She signed the divorce papers in January 1948, citing "incompatibility."

By her own description "an emotional wreck," Diana was invited to live with her friend Kay Hardy, whom she had met in Carmel. A deeply religious woman, Kay inspired Diana to convert to Catholicism. She also found a sense of peace and belonging at the Old Mission in Santa Barbara. It was there that she met a priest named Father Gracian Gabel, who gave her a way to deal with her conflicted feelings about her parents.

"You can love them theologically," he said, "meaning you wish the best for them. But one doesn't always have common interests, even with one's parents. You must *love* them, but you are not compelled to *like* them."

Father Gracian also made Diana the manager of the mission's Serra Gift Shop, which she transformed from a dark room with a few 1920s postcards to a well-lit *two* rooms, attractively decorated and well stocked. With five full-time employees working under her, Diana had transformed the Serra Gift Shop into a considerable source of revenue for the mission. She wanted the shop to offer a series of greeting cards that captured the Spanish baroque period of mission art. The cards would feature a painting of each of the missions' twenty-one patron saints. Inside the card would be a thumbnail history and sketch of the mission. She found the ideal candidate for the job in Brother Solano, a young Cajun man named Bob Cary. The two hit it off right away. In addition to being an expert on art and design, Bob had a buoyant sense of humor and gladly took Diana out dancing once a week.

Bob and Diana married in 1954. Taking up residence in Mexico, they lived a simple but comfortable life, subsisting on their combined incomes from his paintings and her articles. This delicate balance was greatly upset when Diana was told by her doctor that she was pregnant. Their son, Mark, was born in 1961. And if there was one thing Diana was certain of, it was that he was not going to be a child star, not if she could help it.

When Jack Montgomery was terminally ill and approaching his seventieth birthday, Diana decided to give him one last, uniquely satisfying gift. She arranged with John and Dorothy Hampton to host a private afternoon screening of a Baby Peggy feature in their silent movie theatre on Fairfax Avenue in Los Angeles. Diana and nine-month-old Mark took the train from Mexico to Hollywood for the big day. Both of her parents wiped away tears while viewing their beloved actress daughter. At one point, Jack leaned over to forty-year-old Diana and said he wished the film had sound so he could "hear her sweet voice one more time." Marion, looking at her adorable blond-haired, blue-eyed grandson, said to Diana: "Enjoy him while he's young, dear. When kids grow up they're nothing but a pain in the ass."

In 1967, the first volume of Richard Lamparski's *Whatever Became of ...?* Included the story of Baby Peggy. This generated stacks of fan mail for the former child star. Diana took this time to make peace with her screen alter ego. She began talking, not only *about* her, but *to* her. For the adult Diana, Baby Peggy was a separate entity, someone to be spoken of in the third person. What's more, she sympathized with that little girl on the screen. She admired her courage, and despite having been so young when she scaled the heights of the film industry, she retained vivid memories of those very early years. When asked by a reporter if she and Baby Peggy had reconciled, Diana answered, "We get along fine."

Bob, Diana, and Mark eventually moved back to Southern California, specifically San Diego, where Diana was hired as the purchasing agent for the campus bookstore at UCSD. The job, she told me, was stressful, but she found solace in her writing. Her book *Hollywood's Children: An Inside Account of the Child Star Era* contains fascinating accounts of not just her own career but those of her silent and sound counterparts. One of the book's

BABY PEGGY'S 90TH BIRTHDAY PARTY
NOVEMBER 8 & 9, 2008
Edison Theater, Fremont, CA 94536

Diana was honored by the staff of the Niles Essanay Silent Film Museum, a 501(c)(3) non-profit that the silent film veteran faithfully supported. The inscription reads: "For Debbie and Lon. A special one-of-a-kind Birthday remembrance for my one-of-a-kind friendship with you! Love, Diana."

ardent admirers was the stage and screen actor (and former child star) Roddy McDowall. The two became close friends.

In 2003, Bob Cary died, leaving Diana crushed. She left her job at UCSD, and she and Mark settled in Gustine, a small town in the San Joaquin Valley. Mark had been married and divorced, and was granted custody of his daughter, Stephanie, who looked uncannily like Baby Peggy.

One of the best things to happen to Diana—and to silent films in general—is the Niles Essanay Silent Film Museum. Located in the Niles district of Fremont, California, it is the area in which G. M. Anderson, the co-founder (with George K. Spoor) of the Essanay Film Manufacturing Company, produced and starred in 140 one- and two-reelers as the fictional cowboy Broncho Billy. More than 350 westerns, comedies, and contemporary dramas were made in Niles by Essanay from 1913 to 1916. Charlie Chaplin made five out of his fourteen films for Essanay in Niles in 1915, including his seminal comedy-drama *The Tramp*. The studio had a screening room where Anderson and Chaplin watched their dailies. The finished product, and their competition, was seen at the Edison Theatre. The studio was torn down in 1933, but the Edison Theatre remains. Beginning in 2001, the first floor of the two-story building became the headquarters for the museum. Silent films are screened in the theatre on Saturday nights with live piano accompaniment by such renowned musicians as Frederick Hodges. Yearly events, like "Charlie Chaplin Days" and "The Broncho Billy and Friends Film Festival," have also been popular, drawing visitors from all corners of the world. To commemorate the arrival of Essanay in Niles in 1912, historian David Kiehn co-wrote (with Sprague Anderson) and directed a silent film entitled *Broncho Billy and the Bandit's Secret*. It was shot on 35mm black-and-white stock using a 1920s Bell & Howell 2709 hand-cranked camera and all vintage standards and techniques. In addition to the principals, numerous citizens of Niles served as extras, outfitted in authentic period garb. Diana makes a cameo appearance, playing (appropriately) a silent film star. It marked her first appearance in a motion picture since 1938, and her last.

While making the long drive from Eugene, Oregon, to San Diego County to see our family, Deb and I would stop periodically at Diana's home in Gustine. These were no spontaneous drop-ins; we would schedule the visits weeks in advance. Prior to one particular trip, Diana asked what we liked to eat and drink. I said, "Something simple like cold cuts, crackers, and lemonade, but *please*, don't go to too much trouble." She assured me she would not. When we got there, Diana was in an agitated state. Apparently nixing the cold cuts idea, she had decided to step into her kitchen and cook, something she had never really learned how to do. And the results could be deadly.

Deb and I sat at her dining table with our unappetizing lunches before us. "The recipe called for chicken, but I substituted canned tuna fish," she said. That was hardly reassuring. Hoping to put off the consumption of Diana's culinary curiosity, I suggested we first say grace—perhaps in that time a giant meteorite would crash into the earth, sparing us. Deb, who is simply brilliant at ad-libbing prayers, was asked to give the blessing. With the cue of "Amen," and the absence of a meteorite, there was nothing left to do but face the chicken-made-with-tuna casserole. The next sound I heard was a loud *crunch*, followed by the bitter flavor and texture of one of my least favorite substances. Diana confirmed my fear when she said, "Those crunchy things are onions." Using all my self-control, I swallowed what I was eating and even managed to keep it down. Deb looked at me empathetically, but neither of us breathed a discordant word; we would rather risk food poisoning than do anything to hurt this dear lady's feelings. By the time the meal was mercifully over, the success of it had gone to Diana's head.

"This has been so good," she beamed, "I've decided to serve the same thing when the Niles people come by next week."

I silently began to pray for them.

In 2010, I had an idea for a special event, one that would be sponsored by the retirement community at which I held my monthly silent film showings. There would be two screenings of a Baby Peggy feature (a matinee for the public; an evening show for the residents) and our special guest would be Baby Peggy herself. "Just *think* of the publicity," I said. Diana was all for the idea, as was the retirement community's events coordinator. I was given a budget that covered Diana's round-trip airline tickets and a generous speaker's fee.

Because Diana was periodically invited to appear at silent film conventions in the U.S. and abroad, she needed copies of her books to sell and sign. Her autobiography, originally published by St. Martin's Press in 1996, was long out of print. After discussing this with my publisher, Ben Ohmart of BearManor Media, he agreed to republish *What Ever Happened to Baby Peggy?* as a trade paperback, with an all-new cover design. The authoress was thrilled with the results. Now, anytime she needed books, she could order as many as she liked at half price and they would be shipped, at no extra cost to her, to the location of her book signing. I made sure there were two full boxes of books ready for her appearance. I also arranged for the Eugene/Springfield NBC affiliate to send out a photojournalist, Barry Thompson, to cover the event. Deb did her part by securing a guest room at the complex and outfitting it with a deluxe gift basket featuring all the necessities and many of the niceties, including snacks, bottled waters, small containers of Ensure, and some reading material.

I told Diana *The Family Secret* would be the featured film (I had already hosted a screening of the better-known *Captain January*) and that she would be answering the audience's questions afterward. To show you just what a meticulous professional she was, she asked me for the colors of the screening room so that she could coordinate her outfit.

When I went to the Eugene airport to pick her up, she was in a wheelchair being pushed by a flight attendant. She later told me that, at age ninety-four, it was much more convenient for her to traverse the long expanses of an airport by arranging for a wheelchair beforehand. As usual, she was right. It was apparent to me from the outset that Diana was in full work mode. Instead of talking about the things we normally did, like politics, show business gossip, and our day-to-day doings, it was all Baby Peggy all the time. She seemed distracted when the subject veered from her days in the movies, circa 1921 to 1926 (vaudeville also qualified as conversation material). When we took her with us to dinner at a friend's house, I brought along a movie I thought she might enjoy: *Seabiscuit* (2003), a drama about the famed racing horse of the 1930s. As I was about to put in the DVD, she wondered aloud if I had brought along a copy of *The Family Secret*. Not wanting to disappoint her, I drove home, located the disc, and brought it back. As the film was playing and she was adding her commentary, she was back in her element.

The following morning, I went to her room at the complex to see how she was faring. I noticed that every item Deb had placed in her welcome basket was lined up meticulously on a shelf, with each container of Ensure facing label out.

"Where's the paper?" she asked.

"The newspaper?" I said. "I'll go get you one."

"Not a paper," she clarified. "I meant to say a reporter *from* the paper."

"Oh," I said. That was one detail Deb and I had discussed but considered unnecessary. I assured Diana that the news crew would be at the matinee showing. She was somewhat mollified.

Despite the publicity campaign (including a television commercial I recorded), the public showing was only marginally attended. But that evening belonged to the visiting VIP. Deb had arranged with the head chef to create a new entrée, Steak Diana, served with wine. Her carefully selected tablemates represented the crème de la crème of the retirement home's residents. Each of these ladies, who had their hair done and wore their evening finery for this special occasion, were given a signed photograph of Baby Peggy. One of her dining companions, a ninety-six-year-old who expertly provided the film's live piano accompaniment, told Diana that she had the famous Baby Peggy Dutch bob when she was a little girl. Diana, who had heard this kind of thing all her life, smiled sweetly and acted surprised. Observing her was akin to receiving a master class in public relations.

The evening show was wonderfully well received, and the turnout far surpassed the matinee; in fact, the place was packed. So that Diana could gracefully get out of her front-row seat and stand before the audience, I had choreographed the action with her. After making my introduction, I approached her seat in the front row, took both of her hands in mine, and gently helped her to her feet. Once standing, we paused for a moment to allow her to balance herself; I then offered her my arm and we walked to the front of the room. Diana, a professional if ever there was one, made a sly reference to the film's tearjerker ending by rubbing one eye in the style of a child in a silent movie. It was just a small bit, a trifle, but it got a huge reaction. I stood next to her during the question-and-answer session, unobtrusively supplying her with names and dates when her memory faltered.

The final part of the evening involved the selling and signing of books. I'm pleased to say that my regulars did not let me down. As Diana signed, I took the money and put it in an envelope. When the crowd dispersed, every one of the books was sold, and one even had to be specially ordered. It was a great success. The next day, I picked her up and drove her to the airport. Before giving me a farewell hug, she presented me with a copy of her first book, *The Hollywood Posse: The Story of a Gallant Band of Horsemen Who Made Movie History* (Houghton-Mifflin, 1975). I smiled when I read the inscription: "To Lon Davis, a good man to ford the river with."

A week later, I was at the complex when one of my favorite residents, an old gentleman named Howard, asked me, "So, did that Baby Woman make it home okay?"

After hosting Diana, we felt more connected with her than ever. Our friendship was one of mutual support and affection.

When our beloved retired racing greyhound, Bette Davis, died of bone cancer in 2012, this is the letter Diana sent to us:

> Dear, dear friends,
>
> I know how difficult this parting has been for you. But as soon as I learned the sad news, I thought: How wonderful those last years must have been for Bette! After all the cruelty and hardship she had suffered throughout her stormy life, you two caring souls made her last days comfortable and filled with every possible expression of love and devotion.
>
> Having pets is fraught with potential grief because their lives are so short compared to our own. But the exchange of love between you and Bette was 100 percent on both sides. I will remember her as vividly as if she had been my own. You can both rest easy with the thought of what you did for a lost, badly scarred dog of a breed considered passé by most others looking for a companion, and who passersby see as too old to be of use or interest to them. I am so glad you stopped at her pen. You should have no regrets about what more you might have done for her. That's because nothing more was possible.
>
> Bless you both.
>
> Loads of love,
>
> Diana

I stopped in Gustine in 2018 to pay my respects to my darling Diana for what I suspected would be the last time. Within just a few days, she would be celebrating her 100th birthday. It had been quite a while since our most recent conversation. She had gone completely deaf in the interim, obliterating our weekly phone calls. But she seemed as delighted to see me as I was to see her. Despite the hearing obstacle, our rapport was as potent as ever. I knelt in front of her, took her hands in mine, leaned in close, and enunciated so she could easily read my lips. At one point, she told me how much she missed our phone conversations.

"I know what you mean," I said. "I miss them as well."

In all seriousness, she asked, "Why? Have *you* gone deaf too?"

Diana Serra Cary passed away peacefully at home on February 24, 2020, at the age of 101. News outlets around the globe announced her death, accurately stating that she was the last of the silent stars. As per Diana's wish, her cremains were inurned in an outdoor wall at San Carlos Cemetery in Monterey County. Marking her niche are two names, Diana Serra Cary and Baby Peggy. Just as in life, the two share the same space.

Lon and Diana, Gustine, CA, March 2012. Photo by Debra L. Davis.

TEN

Finding Our Niche: A Love Story

I was a child and *she* was a child,
In this kingdom by the sea,
But we loved with a love that was more than love—
I and my Annabel Lee.
—E. A. Poe

*Lon and Debra Davis, Cottage Grove, Oregon, April 1985.
Photo by Charline D. LaCoe.*

Opposites may attract, but similarities keep a couple together. No, I didn't read that in a fortune cookie; it is based on my own experience. In February 1978, when I was eighteen years old, I met twenty-one-year-old Debra LaCoe, a fellow student and employee of the college I attended. Deb and I both had that unmistakable feeling of déjà vu one gets when meeting certain individuals. Had we met somewhere before? Maybe. Just not in this lifetime.

When I told Deb that I was a film collector, she said that she grew up in a home where movies were practically a religion. Her mother, Charline, was discovered by Mary Pickford and Douglas Fairbanks when she was an adorable four-year-old in 1927. Charline might have gone on to have a career as a child star if her grandmother had not turned down the king and queen of Hollywood. Deb also mentioned that her father, Ralph, worked in a camera shop, and that he occasionally rented 16mm prints of silent films to show at family gatherings.

"Which camera shop?" I asked.

"Gailey's on Grand Avenue," she answered.

"That's funny," I said; "I just purchased my new projector from Gailey's."

"Who sold it to you?" she asked.

"A tall man with a crew cut," I said.

"That's my dad."

We just looked at each other and laughed. What were the chances?

Deb graciously invited me over to her apartment for dinner, drinks, and conversation. In addition to mixing a mean cocktail, she is a fabulous cook and an inspired communicator. Before long, there was not a subject that was off limits between us. Instead of a romantic interest, we found in each other a best friend. We established an every-other-week get-together, which allowed us to stay in touch during those hectic college years.

Following graduation, Deb and I dove headlong into a book project I had proposed on Francis X. Bushman. We spent countless hours at the library scouring old newspapers on microfilm; we even took a cross-country trip to Washington, D.C., specifically the Library of Congress, where we pored over original movie trade journals from the 1910s, looking for anything and everything dealing with our subject. Deb, who is a whiz at organization, devised a color-coded filing system for the project. Please bear in mind that this was in 1980 B.C.—before computers that is. During our writing sessions, I would take notes in the now-extinct method known as longhand using a number 2 pencil and an actual piece of paper. Following innumerable rewrites, Deb typed the entire 350-page manuscript on a manual Smith-Corona typewriter. Despite her elevated level of accuracy, there were the inevitable typos; these were repaired with the sensitive application of a globby white fluid known as Liquid Paper. Not wanting Deb to bear this burden alone, I asked her if she would teach me how to type. She did, and because I was so eager to learn, I banged out the phrase "The quick brown fox jumped over the lazy dog" until I became a proficient typist, though still not in Deb's league. Despite the absence of 21st century technology, the skills I learned at that time would benefit my future work as an editor more than all my years of formal schooling combined. I was also working with someone I respected and whose company I relished. We talked and laughed ourselves hoarse every day.

As Los Angeles was only a two-hour drive away, we were able to seek out information from the Academy of Motion Picture Arts and Sciences. We spent several hours in Larry Edmunds Bookshop on Hollywood Boulevard, sifting through stacks of dusty film books and examining the shop's bulging files of movie stills. We even arranged to have three of Francis X. Bushman's long-unseen silent films screened just for us at the MGM studios in Culver City. And we were able to meet and interview various individuals who knew our subject personally, the most important being his widow, Iva Millicent Bushman.

A tiny dynamo in her late eighties, Iva was clearly suspicious of us; she thought we were much too young and far too inexperienced to be her husband's authorized biographers. We set out to prove her wrong. One afternoon, we were permitted to meet with her at her home in Pacific Palisades. And we did not show up empty handed. We brought along a full-course dinner, with a roast, mashed potatoes, vegetables, and a homemade strawberry-rhubarb pie, her personal favorite. Iva, who had once been an actors' agent in Hollywood, never learned to cook. Her oven sat, unused—it had not even been fully assembled yet! To show you what an extraordinary individual Deb is, she put that oven together and proceeded to heat up the meal. Meanwhile, I was in the living room, pouring glass after glass of champagne for Iva.

Deb (right) and Iva Bushman (left) at a meeting for the Francis X. Bushman Futurama club at the Hollywood Knickerbocker Hotel in 1981. The woman in the middle is Lady Grayson, a longtime friend of the club's namesake.

And, boy, could that little lady hold her liquor! I had drained two full bottles before Deb announced that dinner was served. I also took that opportunity to show her the detailed Francis X. Bushman filmography we had been laboriously compiling over the past several months. Well, that officially brought down the walls of Jericho. Iva granted us complete access to her late husband's memorabilia, all of which was stored haphazardly in her garage. And what treasures there were for two eager researchers: Francis's unpublished memoir, ultra-rare movie stills, scripts, several hours of his taped reminiscences, even costumes from his silent films. I felt a direct connection to film history when holding a tarnished belt he had worn as Romeo in the 1916 *Romeo and Juliet*, and the iconic helmet he wore as Messala in *Ben-Hur: A Tale of the Christ* in 1925.

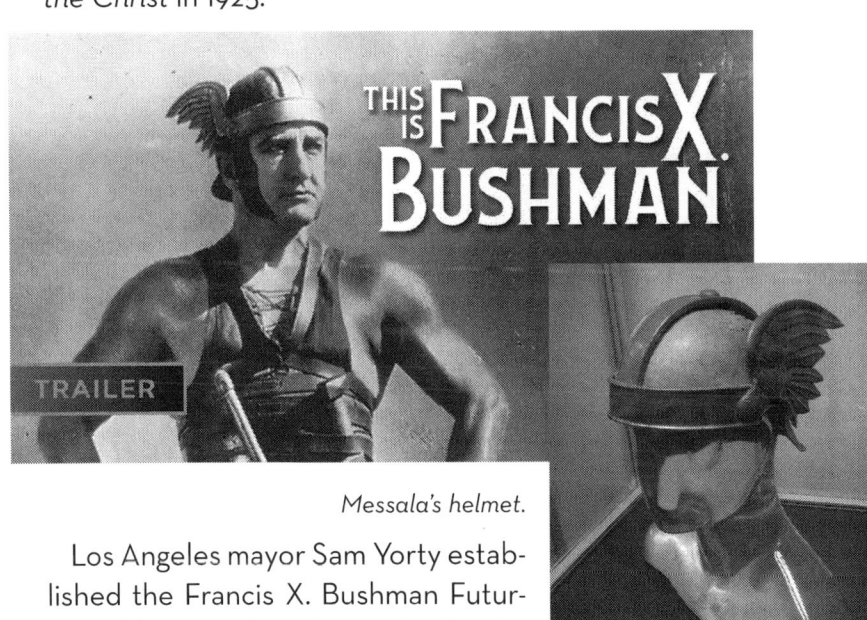

Messala's helmet.

Los Angeles mayor Sam Yorty established the Francis X. Bushman Futurama Club, a cultural organization to honor the actor's memory. Iva was the president of this somewhat eccentric group, which met once a month in a banquet room of the historic (and supposedly haunted) Hollywood Knickerbocker Hotel, which originally opened in 1923. Once a glamorous location frequented by movie stars and popular musicians (both living *and* dead), it had become a stomping ground to indigents, drug addicts, and prostitutes. Order had been more or less restored by the time Deb and I were dutifully attending the meetings, which had nothing—absolutely nothing—to do with Francis X. Bushman. The meetings always began with an invocation by Iva, followed by a spirited rendition of "The Star-Spangled Banner" sung by the entire group. The part of the song that includes the lyrics "And the rockets' red glare, the bombs bursting in air"—the part that everybody has a hard time singing—was always the part the members sang the loudest. Following some announcements, the same dish served at every meeting, Chicken à la King, was passed out by some bored-looking waiters. This was followed by mini-chocolate éclairs, just one to a customer. It was then time for the entertainment portion of the luncheon. Magico of Encino, a teenaged magician who was being sponsored by the group, performed some unremarkable tricks with large silver rings. At another meeting, the special guest was Gordon Gordon, the redundantly named co-author (with his late wife, Mildred) of *Undercover Cat*, an eighteen-year-old novel that was adapted by the Walt Disney studios as the live-action comedy-mystery *That Darn Cat* (1965). Do you remember Jon Provost, the former child actor who played Timmy Martin on CBS-TV's *Lassie*? His mother was the following month's special guest.

One time, as we were making the obligatory drive to Hollywood, we decided that we simply could not bear the pointless tedium of another Futurama meeting. Instead, like two schoolkids playing hooky, we headed straight for Disneyland, where we spent a rainy afternoon repeatedly experiencing the adrenaline rush of Space Mountain. On another Futurama day, we went instead to Buena Park to tour the Movieland Wax Museum, which had a section featuring the waxen doppelgängers of Chaplin, Laurel & Hardy, Ben Turpin, Harry Langdon, Harold Lloyd, and Buster Keaton. There was also a Chamber of Horrors that Deb thought might be fun. She led the way through the darkened corridor as I followed, holding tight to her bra strap beneath her blouse. On still another Futurama day we had lunch at the famous Brown

Derby restaurant, which was located at the corner of Hollywood and Vine. That is the place with the movie star caricatures on the walls; it is also where Lucy Ricardo had that embarrassing run-in with William Holden.

And there were our picnic lunches. Deb would assemble a veritable feast, comprised of fried chicken, dinner rolls, carrot salad, orange slices, chocolate chip cookies, and a chilled bottle of champagne. We would then go somewhere out of the ordinary to enjoy said feast. The Hollywood Bowl, Los Angeles's premier community amphitheater since 1921, was closed for the winter, but we found a way in somehow and dined on the famous bandshell stage. We even had picnics in some of Los Angeles's cemeteries. An especially fascinating one was the rapidly decaying Hollywood Memorial Park, which has since been fully restored and rechristened Hollywood Forever. Located on sixty-two acres in the movie capital, it occupies the same block as Paramount studios and offers a prime view of the landmark HOLLYWOOD sign, with its forty-five-foot-tall letters. Seeing that brought to mind an ambitious but obscure actress by the name of Peg Entwistle. Deeply discouraged by the casting directors who overlooked her, the twenty-four-year-old jumped to her death from atop the letter "H" in 1932.

For many years, the cemetery's biggest draw was Rudolph Valentino, who occupies a crypt in the Cathedral Mausoleum. He was born Rodolfo Pietro Filiberto Raffaele Guglielmi di Valentina d'Antonguolla in Castellaneta, Italy, on May 6, 1895. Growing up in a middle-class family, he dreamed of being a soldier, not a matinee idol. When this did not come to pass, he set his sights on America, and specifically Hollywood. He was cast, usually as a gangster, in several films, and one, *Eyes of Youth* (1919), caught the attention of screenwriter June Mathis. It was she who suggested him for the role of Julio in *The Four Horsemen of the Apocalypse* (1921), directed by Rex Ingram. That same year he co-starred with Agnes Ayres in *The Sheik*, a lurid tale of lust in the desert. Valentino was married twice, both times unsuccessfully. His first wife, actress Jean Acker, locked him out of the bridal suite on their honeymoon night. His second wife, the indomitable set designer Natacha Rambova, took over the management of his career, changing his image, at least temporarily, into that of a foppish dandy. Fortunately, he made up for this tactical error just in time by reprising his über-masculine role in *The Son of the Sheik* (1926). It was while he was promoting that Paramount film that the thirty-one-year-old actor died suddenly on August 23, 1926, a victim of peritonitis. His countless fans around the world were grief-stricken; there were riots; some distraught followers even took their own lives.

June Mathis, ever the good friend, volunteered the crypt she had purchased for her husband, whom she had recently

Rudolph Valentino as The Sheik *(1921). Courtesy of Jerry Murbach (doctormacro.com).*

divorced, as a temporary resting place for the fallen star. It would become his permanent earthly home and one of the most visited celebrity graves of all time. One visitor, known only as "The Lady in Black," wearing a long, ebony veil covering her face, arrived at the cemetery every August 23. She would place a red rose in the attached vase on the crypt, sit contemplatively for a while, and then leave without saying a word to anyone. The mystery lady was later identified as Ditra Flamé. It turns out that the year before he died, Valentino visited her when she was a patient in the hospital. Possessing a sixth sense of his untimely death, he told Miss Flamé, "You are going to outlive me by many years. But one thing is for sure—if I die before you do, please come and stay by me because I do not want to be alone, either. You come and talk to me."

A century later, Valentino still has a loyal following. Each August 23, Hollywood Forever hosts a day-long tribute called "We Never Forget," with a service beginning at 12:10 p.m., the exact time of day he expired. In the evening, fans gather on the Fairbanks Lawn to watch one of Valentino's silent films, projected onto the white wall of the mausoleum.

The mysterious Lady in Black is captured on film by a news photographer sometime in the 1940s. Valentino's crypt is the one adorned by fresh flowers.

Someone Deb and I hold in similar high esteem is the great W.C. Fields. He was born William Claude Dukenfield to "poor but dishonest" parents in a small hotel just outside of Philadelphia, on January 29, 1880. Fields made his initial impact as an eccentric juggler in big-time vaudeville. For a time, he was assisted onstage by his wife, Harriet, whom he called Hattie. When she became pregnant, she decided to quit the act, to her husband's everlasting disapproval. The couple remained legally wed from then on, although there would be no reconciliation. Despite his growing resentment, Fields voluntarily sent a monthly stipend to Hattie and their son, Claude Jr. Meanwhile, the solitary lifestyle of the traveling entertainer weighed heavily on him, and he began to rely more and more on the sedative effects of liquor.

Looking to expand his professional horizons, Fields developed hilarious sketches centered around golf, tennis, and billiards, which he performed to great acclaim in *The Ziegfeld Follies*, beginning in 1915. Fields embodied one of two distinct characters in these sketches. One was a bombastic con artist; the other, a browbeaten family man. He alternated these characters in his silent films as well, although he did not come into his own until the advent of synchronized sound. In the words of his *Follies* co-star Ed Wynn, "A comic says funny things; a comedian says things funny." And truly, Fields was a comedian of the highest order. He was greatly admired by his contemporaries, including his perceived arch-rival, Charlie Chaplin. Speaking grandly out of the side of his mouth, Fields employed a form of speech that was his and his alone. At times harsh, surly, or sarcastic, he could also be sentimental, his voice mellifluous, his vocabulary extravagant. Trademark phrases he uttered, such as "Ah, yes," "My Little Chickadee," "Never Give a Sucker an Even Break," and (his personal favorite) "You Can't Cheat an Honest Man," swiftly entered the lexicon. Making movies in the mid-thirties, a time when the industry's strict production code was in place, it was incumbent on Fields to invent his own form of swearing.

"Godfrey Daniel!" "Mother of Pearl!" "Shadrach, Meshach, and Abednego!"—or merely the well-placed "Drat!"—conveyed his inner fury in a way that tickled the funny bone and quelled the censors. His physical image, that of a now-rotund older man with a boater hat and bulbous nose, frequently turned up in caricature form in comic strips and cartoons. (That big red proboscis was the result of a painful skin condition called Rosacea, which is exacerbated by alcohol. When not properly treated, it can lead to Rhinophyma, which literally means "growth of the nose.")

W.C. Fields, Universal Pictures, 1940. Courtesy of Jerry Murbach (doctormacro.com).

Fields's acolytes have a particular fondness for his more cynical character, that of a child-hating braggart with an insatiable thirst for liquor. In *The Old-Fashioned Way* (1934), he plays The Great McGonigle, the shifty manager of a theatrical touring group. In one scene, Fields's junior nemesis, Baby LeRoy, dips the pompous empresario's gold pocket watch into a jar of molasses. McGonigle gets even with the little brat by kicking his tiny butt when no one is looking. Fields's irreverent comedies would be embraced decades later by the antiauthoritarian youth movement of the late 1960s. A black-and-white poster of a stovepipe-hatted W.C. holding a hand of poker cards close to his vest was a popular decoration in college dorm rooms across the country. At ten years of age I had that same poster on my bedroom wall, at least until my disapproving mother tore it down.

Despite the press's depiction of Fields as an irredeemable misanthrope, I discovered that he was, in truth, far more complex. This insight was given to me by Allen Wood, a character actor who had served as Fields's stooge in the *Earl Carroll Vanities* of 1929. "All those stories about how nasty Fields was, they're not true at all," Allen said. "He was a very generous guy, willing to believe the best about people unless they proved otherwise. After every show, Fields would send Asa, his chauffeur, to the box office with a $100 bill, and Asa would bring back tens. Bill would crumple them up and put them in his pockets. He knew all the old-timers from vaudeville and the stage, and when he met them on the street or at the stage door after the show, he would pass one of those crumpled bills when they shook hands. He did not regard it as charity either. He respected them as fellow professionals who were weathering a bad season, something he had gone through many times himself."

Another rumor about Fields that circulated for umpteen years involved his supposed epitaph. When the comedian was asked by *Vanity Fair* magazine in 1925 what he wanted his tombstone to read, he answered: "Here Lies W.C. Fields. I'd rather be living in Philadelphia." Fields, a Philly native, used the city as a punchline throughout his career. When he is about to be lynched by an angry mob in *My Little Chickadee* (1940), he is asked by the hangman if he has any last words. "I'd like to see Paris before I die," he says. When the onlookers balk at this, he hastily adds, "Philadelphia will do!" In other words, being in his hometown is only preferable to dying! Fields was paid a visit by "The Fellow in the Bright Nightgown"—his colorful term for death—on Christmas Day in 1946, when he was sixty-six years old. From that point on, his proposed epitaph had become so well known that it was widely believed to be true. Still, the question of its veracity gnawed at me. Discussing this subject with Deb, we resolved that one day we would see Fields's grave with our own eyes.

In his will, dated April 28, 1943, Fields had explicitly stated that his body was to be cremated immediately after proper identification was made. Furthermore, he insisted that there be no service of any kind. Why he chose Forest Lawn for his interment is uncertain; he had frequently derided the cemetery for its pretentiousness. When an attorney for Forest Lawn contacted Fields's son Claude and told him of his late father's preferences, Claude dropped the phone and hightailed it to the cemetery. He and his mother were devout Roman Catholics and as such they favored burial over cremation. As a temporary compromise, W.C. was casketed and placed in an ornate crypt, awaiting a judge's decision. In addition, not one, not two, but *three* services were held in his memory. The first was a well-attended non-sectarian funeral at the Church of the Recessional at Forest Lawn. The second, a Catholic Mass, was held at Hattie's insistence. The third and final service, officiated by a female spiritualist practitioner, had been arranged by Carlotta Monti, the comedian's live-in girlfriend for the past fourteen years. Hattie and Carlotta would spend the next several years duking it out in court over the contents of the estate; in the end, the family prevailed, and the girlfriend was left out in the cold. As for W.C. himself, it took three years, but his wish to be cremated was finally granted. Exactly where his ashes were inurned and what his epitaph read was anybody's guess. Hattie and Claude, who had little to no contact with him during his lifetime, were now determined to claim him in death.

Forest Lawn has six locations in the Los Angeles area, including one in the Hollywood Hills. Deb and I toured that location—primarily to pay our respects to Stan Laurel, Buster Keaton, and Snub Pollard—but the flagship of the entire enterprise, Forest Lawn Glendale, is by far the more impressive. Encompassing three hundred-plus acres, it was founded in 1917. The concept of the "memorial park plan" is attributed to one Dr. Hubert Eaton, who strongly believed (*believes?*) in a joyous life after death. His vision for Forest Lawn was that of a garden temple "devoid of misshapen monuments and other signs of earthly death, but filled with towering trees, sweeping lawns, splashing fountains, singing birds, beautiful statuary, and memorial architecture." That vision was fully realized, making Forest Lawn Memorial Park the "Disneyland of Graveyards." Walt Disney himself is interred there, as are Clark Gable and Carole Lombard, George Burns and Gracie Allen, Humphrey Bogart, Jean Harlow, Errol Flynn, Jimmy Stewart, Elizabeth Taylor, and 350,000 less-well-known Angelenos. Part of what appeals to the famous about Forest Lawn is the privacy it affords them after death. Grave hunters receive no assistance from staff members in discovering their whereabouts.

According to the Forest Lawn Visitors Guide, no cameras are permitted on the property, except at funerals. There is to be no loitering, nor is anyone under the age of sixteen allowed on the grounds without adult supervision. Picnicking is prohibited as is alcohol as is feeding the birds as is sitting or lying on any of the park's many benches. Except for the age minimum, Deb and I broke all these rules during our heyday. We picnicked with Spencer Tracy, during which we sat on the bench at his somewhat hidden spot in the Garden of Everlasting Peace (we even shared a plastic cup of champagne with the actor); we photographed Francis X. Bushman's crypt in Freedom Mausoleum's Sanctuary of Gratitude; we even fed a bird or two. Disgraceful, I know. Chalk it up to our being rebellious hooligans in our early twenties.

To see W.C. Fields's grave, we would have to gain access to the Great Mausoleum, the majority of which was, and remains, off-limits to the public. Fortunately, Deb produced a workable plan. It involved posing as potential property buyers who were interested in procuring a joint space, pre-need. To ensure our being taken seriously, Deb insisted we dress the part. She went through my closet and picked out some dress slacks, a button-down shirt, and a necktie. As for Deb, she wore a dress, a pearl necklace, a tasteful pair of earrings, and she looked every inch the lady of means.

On a beautiful spring morning we arrived at the offices of Forest Lawn, housed in charming Tudor-style buildings. After politely inquiring of the receptionist how we might go about purchasing a plot, we were asked to sit in some rather austere high-backed chairs and wait; someone would be with us shortly. Fifteen minutes later, a heavily perfumed middle-aged woman with a can-do attitude arrived on the scene. She was Erica Weidner, a freelance property agent. Deb explained that we were interested in purchasing a joint cremation niche in the Great Mausoleum. Erica drove us there in her late model sedan, all the while filling us in on Forest Lawn's rich history and working overtime to sell us some of its real estate. She also praised what she considered our pragmatism in pursuing a final resting place while still so young. Feeling a tad uncomfortable with all the talk of our imminent demise, I said something to the effect that it would be many decades before our niche would be occupied.

"Well," Erica said, "there's always that other driver on the freeway."

That was sobering.

We told Erica that in addition to finding our niche, we hoped to be able to pay our respects to W.C. Fields. Off the record, did she happen to know where he was? She did, but only vaguely. He was, she said, "at eye level, but hard to find." As she carefully negotiated one of the park's winding roads, we could see a magnificent building rising in the distance. Often likened to Westminster Abbey, the Great Mausoleum is the crown jewel of

The Great Mausoleum, Forest Lawn-Glendale. Photo by Daniel Harrell.

Forest Lawn. It features eleven terraces and more than a hundred stained-glass windows, many from the William Randolph Hearst collection and dating back to the 14th century. Under construction for nearly fifty years, the massive structure contains the same amount of steel and concrete as a seventy-story skyscraper. Seven Michelangelo statues, including The Pietà, were commissioned expressly for the building's Memorial Court of Honor, as was the largest piece there, a stained-glass replica of Leonardo da Vinci's The Last Supper. Although that area is open for daily tours, the part of the Great Mausoleum we were about to visit is the one closed to the public.

Erica led us to the Holly Terrace entrance, where she pressed a button on an intercom. A suspicious-sounding voice answered: "Yes?" Erica murmured something in reply and was immediately rewarded by the metallic *clank* of the door unlatching. She opened it and let Deb and me pass through first. It was as though we had entered an ancient basilica in Rome. What light there was inside was filtered through the stained-glass windows, illuminating the elaborate ceilings. Being allowed inside this august building is considered a rare privilege, one that has been guarded ever more jealously over time. It is a shame really, as there is so much history to be explored! We walked down several flights of stairs until we were deep in the bowels of the mausoleum, where the air is surprisingly warmer and more humid with each descending floor. During that subterranean trek, Deb and I were moved almost to tears by the fascinating objects, including antique toys and hand-written messages, which were placed behind glass-fronted niches containing the cremains of those who were taken far too young. In other areas, there are forgotten works of art that stand in total darkness, their majesty unappreciated.

Back on the main floor, we were making our way down the dimly lit Hall of Inspiration when Erica suddenly exclaimed, "Oh—*here* he is!" Our eyes focused on the tarnished gold-plated plaque in front of us. Due to its size it is more prominent than any of the surrounding niches. It reads, simply, "W.C. Fields 1880–1946," with no mention whatsoever of Philadelphia.

Deb immediately began looking about for vacancies. Located a few yards and two steps down from Fields is the brightly lit Columbarium of Dawn. On the wall next to a tall window were several yet-to-be-claimed one-foot-square niches. Since three is our lucky number, Deb pointed to the third one from the window, on the lowest possible row. She then turned to Erica and asked, "How much would it cost to put us in here?"

Erica quickly checked some figures in a three-ring binder. "Let's see ... five hundred and eighty-five dollars," she said.

"We'll take it!" Deb said.

"Plus, a fifty-two-dollar endowment care deposit."

"We'll *still* take it!"

My jaw must have hit the stone floor. But then that's Deb: when she sees something she knows is right, she does not hesitate. That very day, Monday, March 16, 1981, we co-signed the deed to niche number 30953.

Deb and I continued working together, living together, and basking in each other's company. There would be some major challenges ahead for us, but we always faced them together. When I was in critical condition with a bleeding ulcer in 1982, Deb was with me twenty-four hours a day, sleeping on a cot in my hospital room and seeing to my needs. Her care only intensified upon my return home. Truth to tell, I was not the best patient. I had always been an independent person, one who was loathe to make myself vulnerable to others. Deb, however, knew I needed her help, and despite my protestations she stayed, caring for me until I was well again. It was this level of devotion that caused me to fall in love with her.

One hot summer's night in 1984 we were in our skivvies, swatting mosquitos that had flown in through our apartment's open windows. It was at this unromantic moment that I asked Deb to marry me. Now it was *her* jaw's turn to hit the floor. In the six years we had known each other I never gave the slightest inkling that my feelings toward her had changed. Luckily for me, she accepted. It might have been hot and humid that July, but we no longer noticed. For the next two weeks, our feet—and our hearts—never touched the ground. We were married in a private ceremony that October. Oregon soon became our newly adopted state mostly because we both enjoyed rainy weather. We *still* like rain and we are still very much in love. Just as important, we are still best friends.

What started as a ruse to find the elusive grave of W.C. Fields has become something far more personal and infinitely more meaningful. From time to time we board our cat and drive south a thousand miles to visit family and friends in California. While passing through Los Angeles we invariably stop at Forest Lawn and visit—ourselves. Deb and I typically sit on a marble bench in front of our spot, holding hands and contemplating our life together. It is comforting to know that when our earthly journey has concluded we will be in this historic place, surrounded by beauty and in the eternal company of those motion picture pioneers we so admire. Like all California real estate, property in

Forest Lawn has skyrocketed in the last forty years. According to planning advisor Daniel Harrel, in 2023 our modest niche would sell for no less than $25,000 due to its scarcity and choice location in the mausoleum's corridor/bridge area.

One of our neighbors is Michael Jackson; his sarcophagus is nearby, in the Sanctuary of Ascension. Even closer—in the Columbarium of Dawn proper—is silent film director Fred Niblo and his wife, actress Enid Bennett. One of the original Keystone Kops, Glen Cavender, is there as well. Just a few feet away from us is actor Keenan Wynn and his father Ed Wynn, the great comedian who played the giddy Uncle Albert in *Mary Poppins*; his epitaph is especially touching: "Dear God: Thanks. —Ed Wynn." Believe it or not, a plaque already adorns our niche. Borrowing a passage from Edgar Allan Poe's "Annabel Lee," it reads: "Lon and Debra. We loved with a love that was more than love."

And before exiting the Great Mausoleum, we always stop and give our felicitations to Mister Fields.

Photo by Daniel Harrell.

Index

Abbott & Costello 29, 36, 39, 59, 113
Academy Museum of Motion Pictures (Los Angeles, CA) 96n
Ace in the Saddle, The (Universal, 1919) 139
Ache in Every Stake, An (Columbia, 1941) 97, 99
Across the Continent (Famous Players-Lasky, 1922) 78
Adamson, Ewart 33
Adler, Felix 33
Age of Innocence, The (Warner Bros., 1924) 10, 11
Agee, James 129
All in the Family (CBS-TV series) 46
American Aristocracy (Triangle, 1916) 155
American Film Institute (Washington, D.C.) 17, 140
American Heritage Center at the University of Wyoming (Laramie) 59
Anderson, G.M. (a.k.a. Broncho Billy) 28, 30, 188
Andress, Ursula 45
Ankerich, Michael G. 81
April Fool (Chadwick, 1926) 180
Arbuckle, Minta Durfee 29, 30, 113
Arbuckle, Roscoe "Fatty" 24, 29, 108, 113, 121
Arizona Republic, The 17
Arizona State University (Tempe) 17
Arnold, Jessie 69
Around the World in a Daze (Columbia, 1963) 46
Artist, The (Warner Bros. France, 2011) 166
Astaire, Fred 32
Astor, Mary 30, 138, 162
Atoll K (Franco London, 1951) 88
Aus, Michael (Rare Silent Films) 142

Bafta Award 159
Baggot, King 178
Baker, Eddie 114
Bangville Police (Keystone/Mutual, 1913) 109
Bara, Theda 7
Barlow, Ronald Foster 149-150
Barnaby Jones (CBS-TV series) 13
Bartell Hotel, The (Cottage Grove, OR) 125, 126
Barrymore, Ethel 180
Basquette, Lina 70
Battleship Potemkin (Mosfilm, 1925) 168
Bayne, Beverly 1-22, 64
Bayne, Richard S. 11, 14-15
Beatitudes Campus, The (Phoenix, AZ) 21
Beery, Wallace 14
Bengtson, John 97n, 98, 130
Ben-Hur: A Tale of the Christ (MGM, 1925) 2, 169, 199
Bennett, Enid 213
Benny, Jack 60
Be Reasonable (Sennett/Associated First National, 1921) 112
Berle, Milton 42, 93
Bernhardt, Sarah 146-147
Bettina Loved a Soldier (Universal, 1916) 138
Betz, Audrey 46
Beverly Hills Hotel 117
Big Parade, The (MGM, 1925) 168
Birth of a Nation, The (Epoch, 1915) 87
Blackhawk Films 2, 90, 130
Black Pirate, The (United Artists, 1926) 156
Bletcher, Billy 52, 112, 114, 116
Blues Busters (Allied Artists, 1950) 27
Blythe, Betty 28

Bodeen, DeWitt 91
Bolton, Officer Joe 36
Bow, Clara 138, 178-179
Bragdon, Roberta 17
Brandeis, Madylyn (née Frank) 147, 148
Brenon, Herbert 167-168
Brice, Monte 158, 159
British Film Institute (BFI) 156, 161
Broken Blossoms (United Artists, 1919) 17
Broncho Billy and the Bandit's Secret (2013) 188
Bronson, Betty 168
Brown, Clarence 158
Brown, Dorphia 148
Brown, Joe E. 115, 116
Brownlee, Frank 142
Brownlow, Kevin 122, 130, 153-172
Brownlow, Timothy 165-171
Brownlow, Virginia 162-163
Bruckman, Clyde 33, 121, 131
Bud Abbott and Lou Costello Meet the Keystone Kops (Universal-International, 1955) 113
Burton, Tim 167
Bushman, Francis X. 2, 8-9, 11, 13, 14-15, 19, 21, 161, 197-200
Bushman, Iva (née Richardson) 198-200
Buster Keaton Story, The (Paramount, 1957) 129, 159

Cagney, James 42, 92
Cain, James M. 80
Cannon (CBS-TV series) 13
Canova, Judy 92
Capitol Records Tower 15
Capra, Frank 158
Captain January (Sol Lesser, 1924) 174, 178, 180, 183
Carey, Harry 139
Cary, Bob (Brother Salano) 186, 187, 188
Cary, Diana Serra 173, 174, 185-194

Cary, Mark 186, 187, 188
Cary, Stephanie 188
Cash, Jean 94
Castle Films 90
Cavender, Glen 114, 213
Chaney, Lon 139-140, 159
Chaplin, Charles 4-5, 24, 29, 50, 52, 57, 81, 87, 97n, 108, 117, 117n, 129-130, 154, 158, 159, 170, 170n, 177, 179, 188, 200, 204
Chaplin, Charles Jr. 56
Charge of the Gauchos, The (Ajuria, 1928) 161
CHASE! A Tribute to the Keystone Cops (Davis, eds.) 104
Chatterton, Bob 85-101
Chatterton, Ruth 91
Chisell, Noble "Kid" 115
Cinecon 8 16
Cinephiles Society, The 15
Cineteca del Friuli (Italy) 161
Clarke, Mae 92
Claudia (Franken) 11, 12
Clawson, Elliot J. 142
Clifford, Ruth 141
Cody, "Buffalo" Bill 117
Colonna, Jay 115
Colonna, Jerry 29
Colvig, Vance "Pinto" 114, 116
Conklin, Chester 52, 57, 113, 114, 115, 116
Conrad, William 13
Coogan, Jackie 56, 177, 179, 184
Coogan Law, The 179
Co-operative Theaters chain (Los Angeles, CA) 86-87
Coppola, Carmine 159-160
Coppola, Francis Ford 159-160
Cops (Metro, 1921) 130
Corby, Ellen 45-46
Costello, Dolores 138
Countess from Hong Kong, A (Universal, 1967) 158
Cox, Brady 132
Cox, Melissa Talmadge 131

Cox, Robert 59, 104
Crawford, Joan 32, 138
Crenk, Mary 120
Crisp, Donald 28
Crowd, The (MGM, 1928) 168

Daily Colonial, The (Canadian paper) 146
Dane, Karl 24
Daring and Suffering: A History of the Great Railroad Adventure (Pittenger) 122
Dark Swan, The (Warner Bros., 1924) 78
Darling, Jean 183
Darling of New York, The (Universal, 1923) 178
Darro, Frankie 183
Darnell, Linda 26
Davenport, Dorothy 29
Davies, John Howard 165
Davis, Carl 159, 161, 164, 168-169, 170, 170n
Day of the Locust, The (West) 95
Day, Doris 27
Dempsey, Jack 91
Dent, Vernon 56
Depp, Johnny 167
DeRita, "Curly-Joe" 34, 35, 40-41, 45
DeVore, Dorothy 51, 57
Dodging His Doom (Keystone-Triangle, 1917) 113
Don Q Son of Zorro (United Artists, 1925) 155
Dorothy Chandler Pavilion (Los Angeles, CA) 159
Drake, Tom 92
Dressler, Marie 52, 94

Ebsen, Buddy 13
Edgewater Beach Hotel, The (Chicago) 136
Edison Theatre, The (Niles, CA) 188
Edlin, Theodore (a.k.a. Uncle Ted) 20, 25, 26-28, 59

Edwards, Gus 43
Edwards, Ralph 89
Ed Wood (Buena Vista Pictures, 1994) 168
Essanay Film Manufacturing Company, The 3-5, 17, 28-29, 187, 188
Evergreen (Gaumont British, 1934) 93
Exposition Press 80
EYE Institute (Netherlands) 139

Fairbanks, Douglas 50, 65, 74, 78, 82, 83, 155, 156, 160, 196, 179, 203
Family Secret, The (Universal, 1924) 190, 191
Fax, Jesslyn 45
Fields, W.C. 52, 204-208, 209, 211, 213
Film Chats (lecture series) 87
Fine, Larry (Louis Feinberg) 30-35, 41-44, 45-49
Fine, Mabel (née Haney) 32
Finlayson, James 54, 55
Fishback, Fred C. 176, 177
Fleischmann's Yeast 81
Flowers, Bess 29, 30
For Heaven's Sake (Paramount, 1926) 25, 26
Ford, John 139, 158
Forest Lawn Memorial Park 60, 61, 207-210, 212
Four for Texas (Warner Bros., 1963) 45-46
Fox, Virginia 128
Franklin, Joe 23
Frederick's of Hollywood 96
Friars Club (Beverly Hills, CA) 43
Fulbright, Thomas 64, 82, 83

Gabel, Father Gracian 185
Gance, Abel 155-156, 159-160
Garbo, Greta 158, 159
Garland, Judy (Frances Gumm) 82, 92, 183
Gaynor, Janet 138

General, The (United Artists, 1926) 119, 120, 121-127, 130, 132-134
Gibson Girl, The 6
Gierucki, Paul E. 117n
Gilbert, John 24
Gill, David 130, 159, 163
Girl Shy (Pathé, 1924) 26
Gish, Lillian 13, 50, 73
Go West (MGM, 1925) 52
Golden Age of Comedy, The (20th Century-Fox, 1957) 113
Goldstein, Abe ("Korky") 115
Goldwater's (Phoenix, AZ) 14
Grable, Betty 183
Grauman's Chinese Theatre (Hollywood) 96
Gray, George 116
Great Dictator, The (United Artists, 1940) 169
Gressley, Gene M. 59
Grey, John R. 114
Griffith, D.W. 64, 87, 97, 98, 108, 129, 137, 143, 147, 157
Griffith, Harry 69

Hagen, Jean 30
Hal Roach Studios 88
Hamlet (Shakespeare) 64
Hampton, John and Dorothy 186
Hamrick, Burwell 144
Haney Sisters and Fine 31-32
Hardy, Kay 185
Hardy, Lucille (née Jones) 89, 90
Hardy, Oliver "Babe" 50, 53, 54-55, 57, 86, 87-90, 101
Hathaway, Henry 158
Hats Off! (Roach/Pathé, 1927) 97
Hawks, Howard 158
Hayworth, Rita 26
Healy, Ted 32
Hefner, Hugh 96
Helen's Babies (Sol Lesser, 1924) 178-179
Hennecke, Clarence 114

Her Marriage Vow (Warner Bros., 1924) 11
Herron, Stella Wynne 69
Hersholt, Jean 24
His New Job (Essanay, 1915) 4-5
Hodges, Frederick 188
Hollywood (Photoplay, 1980) 159
Hollywood Cavalcade (20th Century-Fox, 1939) 128
Hollywood Citizen News 82
Hollywood Diary (Lamparski) 91
Hollywood Forever Cemetery 118, 201-203
Hollywood Memorial Park 201
Hollywood Posse (Cary) 192
HOLLYWOOD sign 96, 201
Hollywood Walk of Fame 15, 95-96
Hollywood Wax Museum 96
Hollywood's Children (Cary) 187
Holmes, Christian 81
Holy Cross Cemetery (Los Angeles, CA) 112
Horsley, David 75
Horton, Edward Everett 178
Howard, Curly 32, 33, 34, 35, 36, 40
Howard, Helen (née Schonberger) 37
Howard, Moe 32-38, 60, 129
Howard, Shemp 32, 33, 35, 36, 55-56
Hyams, Joe 14
Hyde Park High School (Chicago, IL) 3

In the Diplomatic Service (Metro, 1916)
Intolerance (Triangle, 1916) 97, 98, 108, 171
Iron Mask, The (United Artists, 1929) 160-161
It's a Mad, Mad, Mad, Mad World (United Artists, 1963) 90
Ivor Novello Award 159

Jackson, Michael 213
James Bond (movie franchise) 13

Jessel, George 43
John Needham's Double (Universal, 1916) 68
Jolson, Al 65, 179
Jones, King Fisher 139
Joslyn, Allyn 30
Joy, Leatrice 5, 16
Julian, Rupert 140-141

Kaiser, Beast of Berlin, The (Universal, 1918) 140
Keaton, Buster (Joseph Frank Keaton) 52, 97n, 115, 119-134, 160, 200, 208
Keaton, Eleanor (née Norris) 128-129, 131
Keaton, Myra (née Cutler) 120
KBSC-TV Channel 52 (Los Angeles, CA) 45
Keith-Orpheum vaudeville circuit 11, 31, 181
Kennedy, President John F. 8
Kennedy, Tom 114
Kenton, Erle C. 113
Kentucky Cinderella, A (Universal, 1917) 138-139
Keystone Kops, The 59, 96, 103, 104, 109-117, 128, 213
Kid, The (First National, 1921) 177
Kingsley, Grace 68, 73-74
Kino Video 160
Kodak Theatre (Hollywood) 163
Kosloff, Maurice 184
Kramer, Stanley 90
Kruger, Otto 29, 30

Lacher, Gary 16, 17, 18, 136
Laemmle, Carl 139, 149, 164, 177
Lakeside Country Club (Los Angeles, CA) 88
Lamour, Dorothy 26
Lamparski, Richard 2, 78, 81, 91, 186
Landau, Martin 167
Lang, Fritz 158
Langdon, Harry 52, 109, 200

Lauder, Sir Harry 180
Laurel & Hardy 49, 53, 54, 55, 57, 58, 86, 87, 88, 200
Laurel, Ida (née Kitaeva) 55, 89, 90, 95
Laurel, Lois Jr. 89
Laurel, Stan (Arthur Stanley Jefferson) 49, 53, 54, 55, 58, 87. 90, 95, 100, 101, 208
Lawlor School, The (Hollywood) 183
Lawrence, Florence 24
Lawson, Stan 115
Lean, David 165
Lederer, Gretchen 142
Lee, Lila 5
Leisen, Mitchell 29
LeRoy, Baby 138, 206
LeVeque, Eddie 103-118
LeVeque, Florence (née Franklin) 117, 118
Library of Congress National Film Registry 69
LIFE magazine 129
Little Pirate, The (Universal, 1917) 141, 142-146
Lloyd, Harold 12, 25, 26, 56, 97n, 157, 158, 159, 200
Lloyd, Harold Jr. 56
Loan Shark, The (Essanay, 1912) 4
London, Babe (Jean Glover) 49-59
Lord, Del 96, 97, 114
Love, Bessie 162
Love Finds a Way (Liberty, 1915) 26
Loves of Queen Elizabeth, The (Famous Players-Lasky, 1912) 147
Luft, Sid 87
Lugosi, Bela 76, 177

MacDonald, Katherine 65, 66, 75, 76-78, 81
MacDonald, Lillian (née Agnew) 65, 66, 76, 77
MacDonald, Miriam 65, 66, 76
Mack Sennett Company, The 96, 104, 112, 176
Mack, Marion 122, 123, 132

MacLaren, Mary (MacDonald) 63-84, 147
Maltese Falcon, The (Warner Bros., 1941) 30
Mann, Hank 115
Mann, Ted 96
Marie, Baby Rose 138
Markey, Enid 5
Mark Strand Theatre, The (NYC) 178
Marsh, Mae 73
Martin, Dean 45, 46
Mary Poppins (Disney, 1964) 213
Matthews, Jessie 93
Mayer, Louis B. 112, 127, 128
McCabe, Prof. John 101
McCarey, Leo 88
McCutcheon, George Barr 19
McDowall, Roddy 90, 188
McPhail, Addie 29
Mead, Taylor 94
Medal for Benny, A (20th Century-Fox, 1945) 26
Meet Me in St. Louis (MGM, 1944) 92
Méliès, Georges 18
Memorable Films Society (Cleveland, OH) 86
Merv Griffin Show, The (CBS-TV series) 15
Metro Pictures Corporation 6
Metro-Goldwyn-Mayer (MGM) 30, 32, 92, 127, 128, 197-198
Midnight Lace (Universal, 1960) 27
Mike Douglas Show, The 37, 43
Minnelli, Vincente 92
Mong, William V. 69
Montgomery, Baby Peggy 138, 173-194
Montgomery, Jack 175, 178, 179, 180, 181, 182, 183, 186
Montgomery, Louise 181, 182, 183
Montgomery, Marion (née Baxter) 175, 181, 182, 183, 186
Motion Picture Directors' Association 67

Motion Picture Home, The 20, 23-28, 27, 42, 57, 112, 157
Motion Picture Relief Fund, The 23, 24, 183
Movieland Wax Museum 115
Movies, Mr. Griffith, and Me, The (Gish/Pinchot) 13
Moving Picture World, The 69, 74, 78, 113, 146
Mr. Laurel and Mr. Hardy (McCabe) 101
Mr. Music (Paramount, 1950) 27
Muddy Romance, A (Keystone/Mutual, 1913) 109
Music Box, The (Roach/MGM, 1932) 88, 97
"My Buddy" (Donaldson/Kahn) 178
"My Dear Girl" (Edlin) 26
My Little Chickadee (Universal, 1940) 206-207
Myra Breckinridge (20th Century-Fox, 1970) 27
Mysterious Mrs. Musselwhite, The (Universal, 1917) 74

Naish, J. Carrol 26
Napoléon (Gaumont, 1927) 155, 159-160, 164, 168, 171
Napoléon: Abel Gance's Classic Film (Brownlow) 159
National Enquirer, The 6
Navigator, The (Metro-Goldwyn, 1924) 121, 130
New York Herald Tribune, The 14, 127
Nicholas and Alexandra (Columbia-Warner, 1971) 13
Niblo, Fred 213
Nickelodeon Theater, The (Los Angeles, CA) 86
Niles Essanay Silent Film Museum 187, 188
Nip and Tuck (Sennett/Pathé, 1923) 112

O'Connor, Donald 129
Old-Fashioned Way, The (Paramount, 1934) 206
Old Mill Farm Store (Cottage Grove, OR) 130
Old Mission, The (Santa Barbara, CA) 185
Old-Time Movie Theater, The (Los Angeles, CA) 86
Oliver Twist (General Film, 1948) 165
Orphans of the Storm (United Artists, 1921) 170
Osborne, Baby Marie 138
Osborne, Robert 91
Our Gang 183, 184
Our Hospitality (Metro, 1923) 132
Our Wife (Roach/MGM, 1931) 53, 54-55

Parade's Gone By ..., The (Brownlow) 159, 160
Paradise Memorial Gardens (Scottsdale, AZ) 22
Paramount Pictures 77, 81, 129, 201, 202
Paramount Theatre (Oakland, CA) 164
Pardey, George A. 120-121
Parker, Albert 156-157
Parsons, Louella 29, 30
Passing Show of 1914, The 65
Passion in a Seaside Slum (Chatterton, 1962) 94-95
Passionate Youth (Truart, 1925) 11
Patton (20th Century Fox, 1970) 13
Peacemaker, The (Liberty, 1915) 26
Peter Pan (Paramount, 1924) 168
Petrova, Madame Olga 5
Pet Shop Boys, The 168
Phoenix Gazette, The 16
Photoplay Magazine 73, 78
Photoplay Productions Ltd. 130, 160-161
Pickford, Mary 5, 24, 73, 158, 179, 196
Picture-Play Magazine 75

Pidgeon, Walter 27
Pierce, David 163
Poe, Edgar Allan 195, 213
Pollard, Snub 208
Poverty Row (Hollywood) 78, 128, 180
Power, Tyrone 13
Preferred Pictures 78
Prevost, Marie 24, 109
Priest, Hal Haig 115, 116-117
Public Enemy, The (Warner Bros., 1931) 92
Purviance, Edna 154
Pussycat Theater, The (Hollywood) 96

Queen of Sheba, The (Fox, 1921) 28

Rae (Bech), Zoe 135-152
Reid, Wallace 29, 78, 176
Republic Pictures 92
Rex Film Company 66
Reynolds, Debbie 27
Rock, Blossom 29, 30
Rogers, Charles "Buddy" 5
Romeo and Juliet (Fox, 1916) 7
Romeo and Juliet (Metro, 1916) 6-7
Romeo and Juliet (Shakespeare) 16
Rooney, Mickey 183
Roosevelt, Franklin Delano 179
Randall, Grace 21, 22
Rosemary Award 64, 83

Safety Last! (Roach/Pathé, 1923) 168-169
San Carlos Cemetery (Monterey County, CA) 194
Santa Anita racetrack 88
Saving the Family Name (Universal, 1917) 74
Schenck, Joseph M. 121, 122, 127
Schulberg, B.P. 78
Scorsese, Martin 162
Scott, George C. 13

Scrambled Brains (Columbia, 1951) 55-56
Screen Extras Guild (SEG) 20, 27
Second Hundred Years, The (Roach/Pathé, 1927) 88
Sennett Bathing Beauties, The 24, 132
Sennett, Mack 24, 33, 54, 57, 87, 96, 104, 108-110, 112-115, 128, 132, 176
Serra Gift Shop, The 185-186
Shannon, Norris 142
Shoes (Universal, 1916) 68-74
Show People (MGM, 1927) 170
Silent Echoes (Bengtson) 97n, 130, 132
Silent Lives (Davis) 132n, 161-162
Singin' in the Rain (MGM, 1952) 30
Slide, Anthony 91
Smalley, Lois (née Weber) 66, 67-69, 73, 74
Smalley, Phillips 66-69
Sombrero Playhouse, The (Phoenix, AZ) 11
Some Like it Hot (United Artists, 1959) 27
Son's (sic) of the Keystone Kops 115
Sondergaard, Gale 95
Soup to Nuts (Fox, 1930) 32
St. Columbia's College 165
St. John, Al 51, 158
Stanbury, Patrick 163
Star Prince, The (The Little Players Company, 1918) 147-148
Steamboat Bill Jr. (MGM, 1928) 127
Stroheim, Erich Von 87
Sul-Te-Wan, Madame 87
Sunset Boulevard (Paramount, 1950) 7
Sutherland, A. Edward 52, 113
Swanson, Gloria 4, 7, 12, 108, 158

Talmadge, Constance "Dutch"
Talmadge, Jim (a.k.a. Buster Keaton Jr.) 131-132
Talmadge, Natalie 130, 131, 132
Talmadge, Norma 131, 132
Talmadge, Peg (née Jose) 131
Taylor, Grace 3-4
Teaching Hickville to Sing (Essanay, 1913) 17, 18
Tenth Woman, The (Warner Bros., 1924) 11
Thames Television 159, 165
"That Lovable Ragtime" (Edlin) 26
Thief Catcher, The (Keystone/Mutual, 1914) 117n
Third Man, The (British-Lion, 1949) 167
This is Francis X. Bushman (Flicker Alley, 2021) 199
This is Your Life (syndicated TV series) 89
Thompson, Barry 190
Thompson, Jim 80
Three Little Beers (Columbia, 1935) 97
Three Musketeers, The (United Artists, 1921) 65, 74, 82
Three Stooges, The 30, 32-37, 48, 49, 55-56, 60, 97, 99, 129, 166
Tillie's Punctured Romance (Keystone/Mutual, 1914) 52
Tillie's Punctured Romance (Christie Bros., 1928) 52
Time of Their Lives, The (Universal, 1946) 95
Titus, Frederick J. 146
Tramp, The (Essanay, 1915) 188
Turner Classic Movies (TCM) 91, 170
TV Guide 46, 55
Twisted Heart, The (MacLaren) 80

Under Royal Patronage (Essanay, 1914) 2, 17, 19
Universal Pictures 66, 68, 69, 76, 77, 78, 110, 113, 138, 139, 140, 142, 148, 149, 164, 177, 178, 179, 205
University of California at San Diego (UCSD) 187

Unsinkable Molly Brown, The (20th Century-Fox, 1964) 27

Van Enger, Charles 140
Variety Arts Club (Los Angeles, CA) 93
Vertigo (Paramount, 1958) 167
Vidor, King 158, 168
Von Sternberg, Josef 158

Wade, Andy 89
Waltons, The (CBS-TV series) 46
WAMPAS Baby Stars 92
Wandering Willies (Sennett/Pathé, 1926) 112
Waterloo Bridge (Universal, 1931) 92
Webster, Harry McRae 3-4
West, Charles 142
West, Mae 27
West, Nathaneal 95
Westminster Abbey 209
Westminster Kennel Club, The 66
What—No Beer? (MGM, 1933) 128
Whatever Became of ...? (Lamparski) 2, 13, 186
What Ever Happened to Baby Jane? (Warner Bros., 1962) 42
What Ever Happened to Baby Peggy? (Cary) 190
When Comedy Was King (20th Century-Fox, 1960) 113
When the Clouds Roll By (Triangle, 1919) 50
Where Are My Children? (Universal, 1916) 68
White, Jules 32, 36, 42, 60, 128
Who Cares (Columbia, 1924) 11
Wilder, Billy 7
Wilshire Police Department 80
Wilson, Elsie Jane 141, 142
Wilson, Lois 5, 16
Winter Garden Theatre, The (Broadway) 65, 179
Withers, Jane 183
Witting, Mattie 70

Witzel Studio, The (Hollywood) 149
Wizard of Oz, The (MGM, 1939) 28
World-Wide Pictures 160
WPIX Channel 11 (NYC) 36
Wray, Fay 138
Wynn, Ed 93, 204, 213
Wynn, Keenan 213

Young, George Herbert 78
Youngson, Robert 113

Zanuck, Darryl F. 128
Ziegfeld, Florenz 204

Made in the USA
Columbia, SC
09 February 2024